E R R A T U M

Yesterday's Clowns by Frank Manchel

The caption on page 143 should read

"Three of America's greatest clown princes in the early thirties; from left to right are Hal Roach, Harold Lloyd, and Will Rogers."

YESTERDAY'S CLOWNS
The Rise of Film Comedy

YESTERDAY'S CLOWNS

The Rise of
Film Comedy

by Frank Manchel

Franklin Watts, Inc., New York·1973

To my dear parents,
HARRY AND PEARL WACHTEL

*"To love for the sake of being
loved is human, but to love for the
sake of loving is angelic."*

ALPHONSE DE LAMARTINE

Photographs courtesy of:
The Bettmann Archive: pp. 37, 40, 41, 60, 68, 69, 70–71, 86–87, 88, 90–91, 92, 93, 113, 114, 117, 118–119, 136, 137, 138–139, 140, 143, 144, 145, 147; Charles Phelps Cushing: p. 17; The Museum of Modern Art, Film Stills Archive: pp. ii, vi, 14, 15, 142; National Film Archive: pp. 16, 36, 38–39, 61, 62–63, 64, 65, 66, 67, 89, 115, 116, 132, 133, 134–135, 141, 146

Library of Congress Cataloging in Publication Data

Manchel, Frank.
    Yesterday's clowns.

    Bibliography: p.
    1. Comedians, American—Biography. 2. Comedy films. I. Title.
PN1998.A2M28   792.2'028'0922   72-7302
ISBN 0-531-02624-8

Printed in the United States of America
5 4 3 2 1

Design by Diana Hrisinko

CONTENTS

Introduction
WHEN COMEDY
WAS BORN

One morning in the fall of 1889, William Dickson and Thomas Edison nervously put the finishing touches to a bulky, wooden cabinet standing more than four feet tall, which they called the Kinetoscope. Eight years of research had come down to this last, crucial test. Dickson inserted the experimental film he had made of himself bowing low and saying "hello." It was a funny bit. The test now was whether or not the routine would be as funny on film as it was in real life. The lights dimmed, and Edison watched as the film was shown on the screen. The great scientist suddenly broke into laughter.

1

The birth of screen comedy came when Fred Ott was filmed
giving his famous sneeze.

Dickson was funny on as well as off the screen. But far more important, the moving-picture toy worked. Edison was now firmly convinced that he should go into the film business. And so it was that film and film comedy began an ideal marriage that is still going strong today.

Since 1889, the art of film comedy has grown to such an extent that it is truly one of the screen's greatest cultural contributions to the twentieth century. One reason may be that the demand for comedy of all kinds is a permanent fixture in society's mind. When life goes sour, people want to laugh; and in good times they still expect their share of joy. It is not unusual, therefore, that the most popular figures in all film history have been the great jesters—like Charlie Chaplin, Harold Lloyd, Mack Sennett, Harry Langdon, Buster Keaton, Stan Laurel and Oliver Hardy, the Keystone Kops, and Hal Roach.

Because of the fantastic changes brought about by the technological revolution, the work of these fabulous personalities has been seen by almost every individual born in this century, regardless of age, geographical boundaries, or social position. For this reason alone, film comedy is an important social institution. In fact, it was the change in society brought about by the industrial revolution that created a demand not only for new and popular forms of entertainment, but also for a new kind of comedy. In place of the traditional rural and aristocratic audiences, there appeared in the nineteenth century a new audience of laborers and factory workers, bookkeepers and clerks, merchants and professional men, who wanted to see *their* values, not those of bygone ages, presented on the stage. And so the successful showmen became those who went into vaudeville, minstrel shows, circuses, musical comedies, and burlesque. These, in turn, affected the style and direction of the more dignified traditional arts. But across the footlights, comedy became the mainstay of entertainment. And with the demand for comedy also came the demand for more clowns, jesters, and comedians. By the time film was born, the stage had trained a whole new generation of funny men.

Even more significant than film comedy as a social institution is the realization that the movies mirror the values and hopes of the people who pay to see them. More is involved than just buying a ticket to laugh. The great comics of the cinema show us as we are and, to a great degree, argue for reforms; they appear to say to their audiences, "Revolt! Society needs to change and these are the reasons why." The comedian's art is based on the differences between what is and what is possible. Through scorn and sarcasm, with irony and satire, they reduce the existing customs and institutions to ruins. Through their comedy, they show us as human beings who sometimes take ourselves too seriously or not seriously enough. Their aim, which has been the aim of all great comedy since the beginning of time, is to criticize the world in the belief that things can be better. In short, film comedy is the cinema's most revolutionary weapon.

The book you are about to read is not so much a detailed history of screen comedy—it is far too short for that—as it is a tender visit with some of the silent screen's greatest comedians. No doubt, you will be struck, as I was, with the fact that so many of them were as pitiable in their private lives as they were funny in their film roles. Throughout, this book will try to illustrate the meaning of Horace Walpole's classic statement, "the world is a comedy to those that think, a tragedy to those that feel." Even then, some memorable stars are left out of this story. For that, I am sorry. My only excuse is that this slim narrative tries to encourage you to read more about *all* of screen comedy.

FM

Burlington, Vermont
July, 1972

The Dandy
MAX LINDER

The first widely acclaimed film comedian was the dapper and amiable Max Linder, who entered motion pictures in the latter half of the first decade of the twentieth century. Although not the first screen comic nor the originator of comedy films, he is generally recognized as the first film jester to develop a unique movie style and win the love of audiences throughout the world.

Born Gabriel Levielle in 1883 to comfortably well-off parents living in the countryside near Bordeaux, France, the handsome youngster soon found himself fascinated with the stage. Encouraged by his teachers and after winning several acting awards, Gabriel left his rustic life to go upon the Paris stage. He did not have much success in the legitimate theater and soon turned to café work and one-night stands. Then in 1905, he met Charles Pathé, often called "the Napoleon of the Cinema."

It was Pathé who had almost single-handedly made France the greatest influence in the film world prior to World War I. Along with his three brothers, Pathé had formed in 1899, the most powerful movie organization in Europe, the So-ciété Pathé Frères, with a red rooster for a trademark. The aggres-sive businessman was determined to dominate the film industry, and in 1900 began building a worldwide network of theaters, studios, and distributing channels. By the time Charles Pathé and Gabriel Levielle met, the former was extremely influential and the latter was looking for some way to maintain himself.

It is possible from today's experiences with movies to for-get just what conditions were like in the early days of film, let alone what film comedy was like. Very few people had any faith in the one-minute, simple-minded novelties that appeared from time to time in traveling shows, store basements, and as parts of vaudeville programs. Next to nothing was known about lighting effects, editing, or acting in the primitive "photoplays"; and the flat, highly inflammable orthochromatic film proved very unreliable to film-makers. To make matters worse, films were exposed in the cameras at sixteen frames per second, and then shown, more often than not, at an unreliable projection speed of twenty-two to twenty-five frames per second. Viewers at the makeshift theaters often watched the crude films shown at abnormal speeds, which not only produced comic effects but also earned the film industry the label of "a low-brow art."

Very few educated or well-to-do people were interested in the "flickers," and even fewer serious actors were willing to appear in them.

It wasn't only the film's infancy that kept actors away. It was also the attitude of the producers themselves. These money men looked upon themselves as the most important people in the industry and kept the public ignorant of the contributions made by the actors, directors, and technicians. Except in rare cases, employees were hired on a day-to-day basis, at very low salaries, and with little concern for their welfare.

The roles that actors took in film required next to no ability at all. The emphasis was on a *moving* picture, rather than on a reenactment of a real life situation. Thus a man staring at nude female statues in a museum was enough to provoke laughter as was a practical joker stepping on a garden hose. No one seemed interested in letting the actor develop *his* relationship to life or objects, to express what *he* felt or desired.

But by 1905, one-minute films had grown into ten-minute films, audiences were getting restless with the constant "movement for movement's sake," and producers were realizing that movies were not just a passing fad. Pathé, in particular, sensed that the fairground days were over and that a new art was on the horizon. He went after creative directors, striking personalities, and a whole new audience that had remained relatively uninvolved with the cinema, those who preferred the legitimate theater—the educated middle and upper classes. His ambitions took him to the respectable artists, to those of the Académie Français, Comédie Français, and to Gabriel Levielle. Pathé convinced the rising young comic that the screen offered him the chance of a lifetime. He could work in films during the day and still perform on the live stage at night. Levielle agreed, but one of the conditions was that he would work under an alias so as not to damage his reputation in the legitimate theater. And thus Max Linder came to movies.

Almost from the start the newcomer gave the cinema a unique star. His peers, for the most part, had sterilized the screen with their emphasis on static tricks and stage-like gestures. But Linder recognized that film comedy could go beyond the artificial and confining elements of the living stage. If he wanted to make fun of a man falling into a lake or off a horse, he could use real locations and animals. He could do what no stage actor could do in the theater. He also wasn't limited by the actual time necessary to act in front of a live audience. Time could be controlled by the artist, not by reality itself. And what's more, through the use of camera placement, the film actor could rely on subtlety and restraint where the stage actor often was limited by what the audience could see and hear past the tenth row. So instead of imitating others, Max Linder originated his famous character, the well-to-do gentleman of aristocratic bearing who calmly faces the world each day in his elegantly tailored clothes, a small mustache, and with a delicate walking cane. No matter what the comic situation, and there were many in the hundreds of films Max wrote and directed from 1905 to 1914, the dandy always lost and regained his precious dignity.

A typical example of Linder's style occurred in his early 1906 film *The Skater's Debut*. The carefree young man tries to ice-skate but becomes not only a menace to himself but a danger to others. Eventually, he is forced to leave the premises. What makes this one-reeler so typical was Linder's emphasis on restrained acting, on building his comedy from a simple situation to a series of gags that give the audience a comic character as well as a good laugh. He demonstrated the way a clever actor could combine his know-how of stage comedy—i.e., precise timing, acrobatic skill, contrast, and exaggeration—with the visual gifts of the cinema—i.e., a variety of camera shots and angles, trick photography, and speeded-up motion. Subtlety and the delicate touch became his trademarks, and audiences everywhere enjoyed this harmless dandy who never acted cruelly, who was always a man of charm, good spirits, and laughter. Here was the kind of comic figure the public could find amusing without themselves becoming uncomfortable. After all, "Max" was a swell who was forced to stoop beneath his social standing, and this made everyone who saw him feel slightly superior. Nothing really important was being criticized. The plots were merely excuses to parade the frivolous Max before us, to give us some gentle laughter without any real significance—in sum, laughter for the sake of laughter.

But Max Linder's fame and fortune were not to last a decade. Europe by 1914 was at war, motion picture production on the continent came to a complete halt, and the ever-fragile Max began his tragic fight with mental illness and physical injury.

Abdominal surgery plus a deep depression about life in general preceded his enlistment in the French army as a private. Although not completely well, the brave patriot soon found himself in some of the bitterest hand-to-hand fights in the front lines, before he was machine-gunned at the First Battle of the Aisne. (Ironically, the Germans, thinking Linder had been killed, sent condolence messages to the Pathé Company.) The wounds forced Max out of combat and into the role of "goodwill" ambassador. But a year later the strain of war and horror caused him to have a mental breakdown and he was confined to a Swiss sanitarium. Still Linder refused to rest and recover, and incredibly convinced the French authorities to return him to combat duty, this time in the air force. Once more the physical effort proved too much for him and the heroic gentleman collapsed. His military service was over.

In the meantime Pathé's influence had spread throughout most of the western world, particularly in Germany, Russia, Italy, and England. Talented comics appeared everywhere to distract their countrymen's attention from war. Only the Americans seemed indifferent to good screen comedies. But appearances are indeed deceiving. In fact, the United States, tutored by the French industry's success, was in the process of refining and developing some of the greatest screen comedies ever.

At the root of their discoveries was America's popular amusements: burlesque and vaudeville. It was here that young comics learned the art of crazy costumes and clever stage properties. To help make the audiences laugh, stage hands used a prop called a "slapstick" to make a loud, slapping sound when the comic told a joke. This was the origin of the term "slapstick" comedy.

By the end of the nineteenth century, visual comedy in popular entertainment was divided into two camps. Burlesque, on the one hand, emphasized risqué and sexual gags. Vaudeville, on the other hand, appealed to the more established, respectable family groups. The talent and tricks of both camps were the same, only the audiences and material differed.

In 1905, when nickelodeons (five-cent movie theaters) first appeared, the kingpins of show business snubbed their noses at the crude toy, patronizingly called "the tape" or "the poor man's amusement." Few realized then how the tables were to be turned. One vaudeville manager, for example, booked that year a popular comedy act—a father, mother, and son team—known as "The Three Keatons," featuring a fresh young kid named "Buster." Also just beginning in vaudeville were such unknowns as Fred Astaire, Al Jolson, W. C. Fields, Eddie Cantor, Fanny Brice, the Marx Brothers, Bert Lahr, and Mae West.

By 1909, more than four million people a day were watching movies, many because they found it cheaper and better than the dollar vaudeville shows. Now, because film was hurting the box-office, vaudeville had to take notice. The first move was to schedule films as "fillers" on the program. But customers soon lost interest in the poor quality of the pictures and stories, and left when they came on the screen. So movies became "chasers," but only to vaudevilleans.

Outside the theater, films were becoming big business. People wanted to see new programs more regularly and movie producers needed new approaches and fresh talent to satisfy their widening audience. It was only a question of time before the infant industry, in its search for performers, would begin to raid the more traditional and popular arts.

Vitagraph, one of the best of the early producing companies, had started with close ties to vaudeville when in 1896 it released its first program of films at Frederick F. Proctor's new Fourteenth Street Theatre. And by the time it was sold to Warner Brothers in 1925, Vitagraph had introduced a number of key people to the screen. The most famous were Rudolph Valentino and the first internationally known American film comedian, the loveable and funny fat man, John Bunny.

Born in New York on September 21, 1863, to British parents who had emigrated to America, John Bunny was a chubby and friendly youngster, dragging himself through Brooklyn public schools with little love for formal education. He found life in a grocery store also dull and ran away to a wandering life on the stage. For over thirty years, he worked in minstrel shows, stock companies, opera houses, Shakespearian plays, and vaudeville circuits. By the time he was forty-seven, he knew that there must be a better way for him to make it to the top. He had faith that this way was in movies. So he went back to Brooklyn, where he had grown up, to the Vitagraph studio in Flatbush and asked for the chance to start a new career. But the producers had doubts. This chunky three-hundred-pounder had been earning $150 a week and had a thirty-week vaudeville contract in his pocket. But Bunny insisted. For nothing, not even a contract, he would give up everything just for the opportunity to work in films. Vitagraph figured it had nothing to lose, so a deal was made for five dollars a day on a temporary basis.

Bunny was an instant success. Audiences loved his funny facial expressions, his stylish manipulation of his large frame, and his subtle gestures. The more popular he became, the harder he worked to polish his style, his scripts, and his films. In particular, John teamed up with the homely but exceptional comedienne Flora Finch, and the two of them created over two hundred comedies about a two-timing husband and his shrewish wife. It was all the stuff that burlesque comedians had used for years, only worked by masters. Here was the roguish husband who was always getting caught stealing a drink, looking at another woman, or sneaking out for some fun with the boys. Nothing in domestic marriages was spared Bunny's humor. He was also quite good at impersonating women or drunks, just for the chance at some exaggerated comedy.

Within two years, by 1912, he was making $30,000 a year and had taken American film comedy out of the amateur class.

His popularity even increased when he went to England to star in a screen production of Charles Dickens' *Pickwick Papers*. Everywhere he went, crowds cheered him and showered him with affection.

When he returned to Vitagraph it was with a renewed dedication to his fans and his work. Until the early part of 1915, he made one fine domestic comedy after another, making fun of the social conventions of marriage and prudish people. But he needed to get away, to relax from the hectic strain of film making. His fans didn't understand. They constantly sought him out and exhausted him in the process. Soon he developed heart and kidney infections which led to Bright's disease. Tired and sick, he became critically ill. Fans all over the world followed in their daily newspapers reports on his fight with death. Then on April 26, 1915, the fight was over and millions everywhere mourned the death of John Bunny. Flora Finch tried to work on her own, but never again gained fame, living out her days in obscurity. But saddest of all, the fat funny man who had made millions for film left only $8,000 in his estate.

It was during this period from 1910 to 1915 that the American film industry was engaged in a great business war, a titanic struggle to see who would gain control of an empire reputed to have over a billion dollars in investments. The main contenders for the prize realized that comedians were the most popular actors with the fans, and the best of them were in vaudeville and burlesque. And so the talent raid began. There was one studio, however, that had a defector from those popular arts, a man who would become the father of American film comedy. They had him and lost him and never recovered from it. For that matter, film comedy was never the same after Mack Sennett came on the scene.

Linder's brief comeback with Essanay in 1917 was helped by his wonderful performance in "Max Wants a Divorce," and the help of Francine Larrimore.

More than any other clown at the turn of the century, Max Linder shaped the future of movie comedy.

John Bunny, the fat comic genius who gave American movies
its first popular film clown, is shown in costume in 1912.

Without question Bert Williams was one of the most gifted
comedians of the early 1900's. It was unforgivable that the
prejudice of the day kept him from making more than
a handful of movies.

The Comedy King of the Pioneers MACK SENNETT

In 1907, the year that nudity became so popular on Broadway with Florenz Ziegfeld's *Follies* and Earl Carroll's *Vanities*, two men left the stage and entered the crude world of "tapes." Both took the same path, first to Edison's Bronx studio and then downtown to Manhattan and the Biograph Company on Fourteenth Street. Neither one knew of the other at the time, but together they pioneered motion picture development. David Wark Griffith came first, and his genius refined the basic techniques of movies to such an extent that he is now widely recognized as the "father of film art." But it was the second man, Mack Sennett, who studied Griffith's methods in cutting, shooting, and constructing movies, who pioneered the great comedy films. More often than not, his moving pictures, by today's standards, seem boring, tasteless, and clumsy. Yet from 1911 to 1932, it was Mack Sennett who was formulating the materials and characters that brought joy and laughter to millions everywhere. And it was this same man who was providing a firm footing in the motion picture world for such stars as Charlie Chaplin, Harold Lloyd, Harry Langdon, Mabel Normand, Ben Turpin, Marie Dressler, and Gloria Swanson.

Born in Canada on January 17, 1870, to hardworking, farming people, Michael Sinnott soon longed for the glamour of the stage. His family, for years, tried to discourage him. Then, when he was seventeen, the Sinnotts moved to East Berlin, Connecticut. While Michael, his father, and two brothers worked as boilermakers and ironworkers, his mother and sister ran a boarding house. One of their tenants was a music teacher who convinced the proud woman that her son had musical talent. A deal was arranged. Catherine agreed to give the teacher free room and board in return for his giving her son free lessons in the evening.

One year in Connecticut was enough to convince the ex-Canadian farmers that they had a better future in Northampton, Massachusetts. And it was there that the would-be opera singer persuaded his mother to get him a letter of introduction to a visiting actress who, in turn, might get him a start on Broadway. So Catherine Sinnott asked the family's twenty-nine-year-old attorney, Calvin Coolidge, later to become the thirtieth President of the United States, to write a letter of introduction to Marie Dressler. This famous stage star, whom twelve years later Sennett would launch on a great film career, was fascinated with the ambitious eighteen-year-old strong boy, whom she called "Rivets," and wrote a letter for him to one of the stage's most powerful producers, David Belasco. With Miss Dressler's letter in hand, Mike, in 1902, left for New York and the big time.

But neither Belasco nor Broadway had much use for a stocky Irish bass who couldn't dance and had almost no stage experience. Besides, no one wanted an actor whose name sounded like "Snott!" So Mike became Mack Sennett and decided to learn the hard way, in the burlesque houses on New York's Bowery.

While burlesque taught people the facts of life the hard way, it was also the proving grounds for many of show business's greatest stars. There among the slapstick comedians and the fat dancing girls, in spite of the obscenity and immorality, the inexperienced youth studied acting and comedy. He learned, for example, to accept people for what they were, to ridicule authority and pretension, to thumb his nose at society's foolish sex taboos, and to survive audiences, who, when they didn't like your act, booed, hissed, jeered, and belted you with rotten fruit and vegetables. He also learned how to create *visual* comedy, to make people laugh because of ridiculous clothes, oversized shoes, baggy pants, and alcoholic red putty noses. Over and over again burlesque proved that nothing is so sacred that it can't be a source for comedy, that people prefer to laugh rather than cry, and nothing makes the average man in the audience happier than to feel superior to others. Most of all, Mack Sennett discovered that he was more interested in jokes than in songs.

Over the next five years, he tried a number of roads to the top: circuses, vaudeville shows, variety acts, and even the theatrical stage itself. But by 1908, Mack found himself throwing in his fortunes with the film makers of Biograph. At the start, he was unhappy with his acting roles and never socialized much with the other members of the company. Griffith, however, appealed to him. He liked the director's assurance and his obvious talent; and Sennett, determined to succeed in this new field, invented ways to get close to the rising artist. Sometimes he carried the director's camera, at other times he just happened to be walking Griffith's way.

Nothing dramatic happened in the two years that followed. The ex-Canadian farm boy appeared in close to a hundred films, mostly melodramas, and his acting, to be kind, was acceptable.

But the film audiences began demanding longer films. Instead of the usual ten minutes, people wanted twelve-minute shows. The producers balked at changes of any kind. To pacify the fans, they kept the dramas at the standard 850 feet of film, but began making short comedies, "split-reels," about 100 to 125 feet. These split-reels were then added to the dramas and a twelve-minute show resulted.

By now, Sennett wisely realized that his future in film lay behind instead of in front of the camera. He pleaded with the studio officials to let him direct comedy pictures, but no one was interested in "fillers," except as additional material to the serious, sentimental movie stories.

Then, in the summer of 1911, one of Biograph's directors became ill and the studio needed someone to help Griffith in making pictures. Sennett got the assignment.

Right from the beginning the great film pioneer set out to ridicule the popular, sentimental screen stories of the day. His brash and roughhouse pictures specialized in poking fun at people in general, regardless of their size, importance, or looks. What's more, Sennett made it appear so easy. The stories had simple, straightforward plots where people became confused, misunderstood, and eventually manhandled, more often than not, by a swift kick on the backside.

By the end of the year, Mack had made more than fifty comedies. Far more important, however, he had assembled around him the beginnings of a long list of memorable talent. One key figure was Henry Lehrman, who in later years became one of Sennett's greatest comedy rivals and personal enemy. Legend has it that Henry wanted to be an actor and was under the impression that studios liked people with experience in French films. So he appeared one day at Biograph and announced that he was a former Pathé employee. No one was fooled by his phony French accent, but Griffith was shooting a scene of a last-minute rescue from a burning building, needed some extra players, and gave Henry a chance to show his stuff. Excited, the inexperienced actor ran up the stairs and threw himself madly out of the second-story window. Unfortunately, the cameraman missed the whole bit. That didn't bother Henry. He did it all over again. His enthusiasm earned him a job and the name "Pathé" Lehrman.

Another member of Sennett's comedy unit was Fred Mace, an ex-dentist who felt that thirteen months of filling cavities was enough for a lifetime and fled to a career of clowning in stock and musical companies. His specialty was playing "fat man" parts, and in 1911 he came to Biograph, made some films for them in California, and decided to remain in Los Angeles when the company returned to New York. But Fred had made a strong impression on Sennett, and Mack knew it was only a matter of time before they would be back together.

The third key figure was Ford Sterling, a tall, athletic ex-clown who arrived at Biograph the same year as Mace, 1911. He had some minor fame as a clown in vaudeville and musical comedy, specializing in knockabout roles that called for a stupid villain to be outwitted by a smaller and cleverer man. Now he too wanted to act in comedy films.

But of all the Biograph comics, the most important turned out to be a sixteen-year-old model who had returned after a two-year absence from the studio. She was lovely, warm-hearted, and a natural mimic. She reportedly ate ice cream for breakfast while reading classic novels. What's more, Mabel Normand became Mack's girl friend. In the years to come, she would be known as "the female Chaplin."

At the end of 1911, Sennett discovered that although Griffith had the reputation, Mack was the studio's big money-maker. It was about that time that two ex-bookmakers became interested in this funny, thirty-one-year-old director.

Adam Kessel and Charles Baumann, petty gamblers, had gone into the motion picture business when one of their customers couldn't pay his debt and gave them several cans of film in exchange. By 1910, they owned the New York Motion Picture Company, which had two producing units: The Reliance Company in the East, for making dramas; and The Bison Company in the West, for making westerns. In 1912, having scouted Sennett's work, Kessel and Baumann approached Mack and offered to set up a third company, in California, to make comedies. Sennett gladly agreed to head the new *Keystone* organization. He would own a third of the company, and get a $100-a-week salary. But best of all, he could make his own brand of comedies with his own actors.

Although the decision to form Keystone was made in January, the company did not begin operations until the summer.

The delay came as the result of a legal fight between Kessel and Baumann and Universal Pictures. The final settlement required the ex-bookmakers to pay a large sum of money and give up the trade name of Bison Pictures. This done, they took their cowboy director, Tom Ince, and gave him a new studio. This freed his old studio, Edendale, a former grocery store, for Keystone Comedies. The legal battle also brought Fred Mace back to Sennett. In the meantime, Mack, without any material, money, or equipment, was convincing Mabel Normand, Ford Sterling, and Henry Lehrman to follow him to Hollywood.

The first Keystone comedies were released in August and by the middle of 1913, with more than a hundred in circulation, Sennett films were the favorite fun pictures of exhibitors and audiences everywhere. The blueprint for most of the outstanding comedians and comic films of the future had started. Behind Keystone's success was the guiding hand of this unusual man, Mack Sennett, who, in fact, was more a master of ceremonies than a performing artist. His genius lay in blending the best of burlesque with the art of the silent film. He hadn't originated film slapstick, as Griffith hadn't created cinematic technique; but, like Griffith, he perfected what other men had only stumbled on.

One method Sennett used was to encourage his performers to develop inhuman characterizations, types that seemed never to show pain, emotion, or human feelings. The idea of knockabout comedy, with its emphasis on make-believe fights, falls, and accidents, was to get people to laugh without being worried about the welfare of the actors. The performers, therefore, had to steel themselves against any outward reaction to physical punishment. This they did by training in acrobatics, bizarre makeup, and funny costumes, plus split-second timing. Ford Sterling specialized in stereotyped Jewish and Dutch roles, Fred

Mace popularized fat Spaniard stereotypes; and everyone on the lot took a turn in blackface and female impersonations.

The most famous characterizations, however, were the Keystone Kops, the zaniest patrolmen ever. In charge was Sterling, as Chief Teheezal, a man whose every order was disobeyed or misunderstood. And with him over the years were most of the studio's comedians. This was because Sennett wanted tough actors who knew how to survive serious falls and work with aching bones. No better test course ever existed than taking a trial ride with the Keystone Kops in their crazy patrol wagon that raced across the screen like greased lightning going nowhere fast.

There was one gag—falling off on your rump while the paddy wagon was moving—that few dared try. Legend has it that when Ben Turpin, the great cross-eyed wonder, asked Sennett for a job, the boss, being superstitious, put him to work as a janitor. After a brief period, Mack agreed to let Ben take a trial run with the Kops. The wagon started with Turpin as last man on, and then suddenly he began bouncing off and on, off and on, in the most hilarious manner. Soon it became a contest who could fall better, but for Ben Turpin it was the beginning of a wonderful career. His specialty became doing a 108—a burlesque fall where the actor puts one foot forward, the other behind, then doing a counter somersault lands flat on his back. He was one of the few screen jesters to save his money, have a happy life, and retire in comfort. His favorite pastime in later years was to direct traffic at the height of the rush hour in downtown Los Angeles. His wildly swinging arms and crossed eyes caused more confusion than most riots.

Another unique feature of the Keystone comedies was the way they were created. Sennett had a great love for bathtubs and an equally great fear that his employees took advantage of him. His solution was to erect a tower in the center of the studio lot so he could not only spy on his underlings, but also take a rub-down in a giant marble tub he had built for himself. Usually the films began when one of his writers came to the tower with a simple plot for a picture. Each plot had to be explained to Sennett in pantomime for him to see. (Mack believed if you couldn't act out the idea, you couldn't film it.) After making his standard changes in someone else's story, Sennett and the writer went to the top of the tower, where six men were "locked" in a gag room without telephones, books, or magazines. There, behind closed doors, the gag men considered a number of funny things that could happen in a simple setting with uninhibited actors. Afterwards they gave some brief sketch to the director, but no script. All Sennett pictures had to be shot from memory.

The Surf Girl, made in 1916 when Sennett had hit his peak, is a good example of how the master combined visual, roughhouse comedy with silent film artistry. The setting is a beach where a number of different people come for fun and relaxation: a couple dating, a henpecked husband, his shrewish wife and their adventuresome daughter. The gag writers set up a number of attractions: a swimming pool, a roller coaster, a ferris wheel, a beer hall, a dressing room, the ocean, an amusement park, and a large cage of ostriches. Then they quickly set things in motion with a "plant," a cause for confusion. The girl wanders innocently into the swimming pool area where her strong-arm boyfriend tests his strength at "the hammer and bell" game. The father meets a friend and sneaks off to have some fun. All this in the opening feet of the two-reeler. Then the plants were added: the boyfriend mistakes another man's intentions towards his girl, the shrewish wife goes after her wandering husband, and the curious daughter decides to flirt with some lifeguards. What results is a Pandora's box of wild, physical comedy: fights, riots, accidents, chases, and madcap rescues. Not only the central characters, but also innocent bystanders are soaked, assaulted, chased, and humiliated. Sprinkled throughout are special camera effects like reversing the film so that you get the impression swimmers are flying out of the pool when a fat man slides in, or undercranking the camera to shoot fewer frames of the action so when the scene is projected on the screen the action is speeded up: people run faster, swim more quickly, and seem more ridiculous.

This slapstick two-reeler is the kind of "riffing"—an assortment of gags—that audiences came to expect from Sennett. Others imitated him but few understood what he had learned from Griffith: the concept of "tempo." It was this concept he applied to comedy films. Gags in themselves were not funny, Sennett reasoned. It was the context in which they were shown and the time that elapsed between them that was so crucial. Put your best gag first and the others seem flat and trite. Put your gags too close together and the audience is going to miss some of them. Take too much time between them and your audience becomes bored. The secret was pace—so much time to laugh, to settle down, to laugh again.

Sennett also knew what made the average man in the audience laugh. Burlesque had taught him about slapstick humor, and no film ever got shown to the public that didn't first make Mack laugh. What this meant was that the films had to be populated with absurd and grotesque comic types: the fat, the skinny, the shy, the boastful, the tall, the short, the fool, the smarty-pants, the rich, the poor. And each of these extreme types had to become tangled up very quickly in an ever-increasing set of fights, feuds, and frustrating situations that ended in a zany and perilous chase.

28

The emphasis on "chases" was Keystone's third unique feature. Again he had studied how Griffith's expert cutting had transformed French standard chase scenes into exciting moments of suspense and tension. Mack sensed that if pursuit made for good drama, than a parody of it made for excellent comedy. So every film from the "fun factory" ended with a frantic chase in which absurd people pursued each other with bombs and bullets, trains, cars, and planes, more often than not colliding and crashing in one incredible crack-up. But the customers adored it. The actors never appeared hurt. It was, as one critic noted, like playing with mechanical toys that bounced off each other just in fun.

Still another aspect of Sennett's genius was his use of bathing beauties. It seems that in the early days of Keystone his publicity men had trouble getting free advertising for the comedians in the newspapers. No matter how weird their stunts, editors paid little attention to Sennett's funny men. Then one day, according to legend, Mack read about a minor accident that was given a lot of attention because a lovely girl was involved. He remembered how he and Mabel had once made a successful swimming film at Biograph and he decided to hire some pretty girls for Keystone, put them in bathing suits, and get some publicity. The idea worked. Not only editors but film audiences enjoyed watching the good-looking girls in "risqué" suits who rarely went into the water. So Sennett's bathing beauties became a fixture at the studio. Many of the girls eventually went on to do other things; the most famous was the great silent screen star Gloria Swanson.

Of all Sennett's contributions, most people remember his fascination with pie-throwing. No one knows for sure how it started, but the honor seems to belong to Mabel Normand. The story is told how in 1913 the clowns were making a movie with the loveable fat man Roscoe Arbuckle and nothing seemed funny. Try as they would, every gag fell flat. Mabel, who was not in the scene, sat by watching, bored, when she spied a pie lying nearby. Since they were all practical jokers, Mabel, quite naturally, picked up the pie (no one knows what kind) and heaved it at Roscoe's face. Instant laughter resulted. And no Sennett comic after that ever failed to learn how to pitch pies. Few outside the studio, however, learned the art, mainly because they used regular pies which did not have the right ingredients to maintain themselves while airborne.

Imagine what it must have been like to be a visitor at this fun factory. Sennett arriving at work about 8 A.M. on horseback; actors belting each other with fake bats, clubs, bottles, bricks, pies, and anything that moved. Cars and motorcycles, buildings and stores getting destroyed. And no one ever was sure what was to come next. Yet, in the midst of this bedlam, high up in the main tower, Mack Sennett was either getting a rub-down from his masseur, taking a bath, or spying on his employees.

Balanced against Sennett's many strengths were some glaring weaknesses. Not only did actors have trouble pleasing the tyrannical film maker, but even those who obeyed his excessive orders rarely got paid what they were worth. Almost all of his stars came to him for better parts and higher salaries and found to their dismay that their choice was acceptance of Sennett's terms or go to work elsewhere. Lesser performers lived on a day-to-day existence, because Keystone for many years refused to give contracts. This way if weather was bad, filming could be cancelled and expenses were kept down by not having to pay idle actors who couldn't work that day. (Studio lighting had yet to be fully developed.) Each of the famous people who started with Sennett left for special reasons, but the saddest story was Mabel Normand's.

Sennett had loved her for many years and both of them always talked about marriage but never set an exact date. Finally in 1915 they decided that it was time and picked July 4th for the ceremony. But a month before the appointed time Mabel caught him with another woman. He claimed she misunderstood, that he was doing nothing wrong, but Mabel would not believe him. The engagement was broken.

About that same time, Kessel and Baumann joined with other producers to form a new company, Triangle, with Griffith, Ince, and Sennett as the three major directors. Mack used this opportunity to convince his backers that Mabel should have a producing unit of her own, which they agreed to form. By now, the great actress had turned to drugs and alcohol as cures for her loneliness and sadness.

Mabel chose for her new film the story of a poor girl who becomes a modern cinderella. It was a wonderful performance, but it took eight months to make and cost more than a quarter of a million dollars. What's more, Mabel added a touching tenderness to her usual comic role. When Kessel and Baumann previewed *Mickey,* they became very angry. The producers didn't appreciate the actress's new style and refused to release it, calling the picture "Sennett's Folly." Some months later, so legend has it, a Long Island exhibitor called the Triangle's rental offices complaining that his Saturday night film hadn't arrived. The clerk, new and inexperienced in these matters, went to the film room, took the first can of pictures he found, which happened to be *Mickey,* and rushed it over to the theater owner. Suddenly, *Mickey* became an overnight sensation. Fans were yelling that Mabel Normand was greater than ever.

But her sudden popularity was of no use to Kessel, Baumann, and Sennett. When Mabel learned that *Mickey* had been "shelved," she had quit the company and gone to work for Samuel Goldwyn.

During the next few years, the great comedienne's life began to take a turn for the worse. A wild social life plus drugs and drink had made her nervous, cranky, and difficult to work with. Newspaper after newspaper printed rumors about "Madcap" Mabel coming late to work, fighting with directors, and complaining about Goldwyn pictures in general. Then in 1920, she disappeared from a film set and turned up in Europe, on a mad spending spree. When she returned, friends were so envious of her wardrobe that she turned around and took her friends to Paris to outfit them. The cost of this escapade approached the million dollar mark and a fickle public began to reconsider its estimate of this reckless film star. To make matters worse, on returning to America, Mabel had to be institutionalized for drug addiction.

Although the cure failed, Mabel left the sanitarium and began making films with Sennett again. Mack, still deeply in love with her, gave her a contract and wrote a special screenplay entitled *Molly-O,* another cinderella story. This was to be his last chance to win her back. By the end of 1921, the film was finished and ready for release early in 1922. In the meantime, the tragic Mabel started work on her next movie, *Suzanna,* a comedy about love in Old California.

In the evenings she occupied herself with a homestudy program of serious books. This interest had started a friendship between Mabel and a Paramount film director named William Desmond Taylor. On January 31, 1922, he called her, stating that there was a book he wanted her to read and would she stop by his house to pick it up. Later that day, her chauffeur drove Mabel to Taylor's home. The valet let her in. Taylor was on the phone, having a heated discussion. She waited a few minutes, he finished his conversation, and then the two of them talked for about a half-hour in the living room. Then Taylor took Mabel to her car, said good-bye, and went back into the house. The next morning when the valet reported for work, he found William Desmond Taylor lying on the floor murdered! Mabel Normand had been the last known person to see him alive.

The case of who murdered Taylor was never solved. But the circumstances around it became sordid. Mary Miles Minter, an adolescent star, screamed hysterically that Taylor, twenty-four years her senior, and she were to be married. Investigations revealed that he had deserted a wife and child in the East. What this had to do with Mabel Normand, no one today understands. But the public, who had adored her, suddenly decided that guilt by association was enough to destroy "Madcap" Mabel. Yellow journalism fed their hate and people began avoiding Normand movies.

Sennett stood by her (so did Chaplin, Valentino, and Keaton). In 1923, Mack released *Suzanna* and Mabel's final film for him, *The Extra Girl,* a witty story about a hard-luck actress. But fortune had fled from Mabel Normand. During 1923 she had attracted the attentions of a wealthy playboy and in the early hours of New Year's Eve, he came to her house demanding that she go out with him. Mabel's new chauffeur came to her rescue, pushed the man outside the house, and then in the darkness, several gun shots were heard. It turned out that Joe Kelly, the driver, had wounded the playboy (who recovered), but the newspapers made a big thing that Kelly's real name was Joe Greer, escaped convict and dope addict. He was acquitted for the shooting, proving self-defense. But once more Mabel Normand was involved in scandal. The public did not forgive her, and for all practical purposes her screen career was over. Although Sennett still wanted to stand by her, this time Mabel refused. She saw no point in having him destroyed along with her. And so they parted for the last time.

On the night of September 28, 1926, at a dinner party she gave for a number of friends, Lew Cody, a colleague from her Biograph days, proposed marriage and, on a dare, she accepted. By five A.M. they were man and wife. Sennett never forgave her for marrying someone else; he remained a bachelor all his life. As for the newlyweds, they were man and wife in name only. Their professional lives kept them separated for most of the time.

In 1929, while they were apart from each other, Lew and Mabel developed fatal illnesses: he, a heart condition; she, tuberculosis. Neither one wanted to be a burden to the other so they kept their problems a secret. But before the year was finished, the couple was reunited in California and their secrets were apparent to everyone. Lew moved to a nearby hotel to conserve Mabel's strength. Nothing helped. In January she had to be taken to a sanitarium for professional care. Then on February 23, 1930, at thirty-four years of age, one of Hollywood's most gifted comediennes died.

Mabel Normand was just one of many who gave Sennett premature white hair one year after he took over the Keystone Company. Fred Mace was another. His popularity with fans skyrocketed in 1912 and by April, 1913, he had quit Sennett to form his own company to compete with John Bunny and Max Linder. But without Mack's guiding genius, Mace was lost. Sennett took him back in 1915, but by then Fred was a has-been and within eighteen months he was on his own again. Shortly thereafter, while in New York City, presumably to start a new job, the thirty-eight-year-old actor died suddenly. Some claimed it was a heart attack, but others rumored that Mace took his own life because he felt there was nothing left to live for.

Fred Mace, to some degree, opened the door for two of Sennett's greatest stars. The first was Roscoe "Fatty" Arbuckle. When Mace left Keystone in 1913, the company needed a new "fat man" to take his parts. Mabel Normand convinced Sennett that Roscoe, an unemployed comic from vaudeville and musical comedy, would be perfect. He was a hard worker, fat, and very funny. She proved to be right. Within a very short time "Fatty" Arbuckle and "Madcap" Mabel became extremely popular as a comedy team.

"Fatty's" popularity and Fred Mace's success in 1913 made Ford Sterling so jealous that he began giving Sennett a hard time. The more Mack refused his demands, the more Ford resented his former friend. Finally he let it be known that he was leaving Keystone.

As always, Sennett accepted the inevitable. Now the question became who would take over Sterling's roles. By coincidence, Mack remembered an evening Mabel and he had spent at William Morris's Forty-Second vaudeville theater earlier that year. (That is the same William Morris who later became head of one of America's greatest talent agencies.) The couple had been impressed by Fred Karno's English touring company. In particular, there was a bit called "A Night in an English Music Hall," in which a short man, dressed as a gentleman and acting drunk, continued to annoy the performers. The "Limey" was very funny and very clever. Mack remembered him now when Sterling was preparing to leave Keystone. Being in California, Sennett wired back East for Kessel to hire the little fellow called "Chapman" or "Champion." It was a request that gave motion pictures its greatest star.

Mack Sennett, the ex-boilermaker who became the father of film comedy.

Mabel Normand, the greatest comedienne in motion picture history.

Some of Sennett's most famous comics are shown in this classic from right to left are "Fatty" Arbuckle,

shot of the Keystone Kops: Ford Sterling is seated at the desk and
Rube Miller, Hank Mann, and Al St. John.

Ben Turpin, the cross-eyed wonder, who loved to make fun of everyone. In this scene from "The Sheik of Araby" (1923), he does a takeoff on Rudolph Valentino.

Sennett often paired his great stars as comedy teams. Here is a scene from the popular series featuring Arbuckle and Normand. The film was "Fatty and Mabel Adrift" (1916).

The Master Clown
CHARLES CHAPLIN

It was in early May, 1913, that Kessel finally located Fred Karno's touring company at a Philadelphia theater. By luck, Charles Chaplin was backstage when a telegram arrived, seeking information about the "drunken" comic. Since New York was less than three hours away by train, the young man agreed to come to the producer's Broadway offices to discuss a business deal. After listening to the movie proposition, Chaplin weighed the pros and cons of leaving the stage. True, he was fascinated by the new form of comedy, but Charles didn't think Keystone's crude and senseless slapstick offered him much of a future. The chance of making films, however, might increase his reputation with audiences and if things didn't work out in Hollywood, he could always return to the music halls, the English version of vaudeville, a bigger star than he was now. That possibility decided the issue. And so for $150 a week, twice as much as he got from Karno, Chaplin accepted a year's contract with the Keystone Company. The one reservation was that he couldn't begin until the end of 1913 when his recent contract ended.

By 1916, the shy, inexperienced film actor had developed into the screen's funniest clown. After that, critics and audiences alike for the next fifty years acclaimed him the greatest entertainer of the twentieth century. And yet it was to be the years before he came to the movies that so significantly shaped his fabulous career and stormy private life.

Charles Spencer Chaplin, Jr., was born in London on April 16, 1889; his parents were struggling music hall performers who probably never knew that Edison in America was giving birth to a new art form in the shape of the kinetoscope. Chaplin, Sr., was a fading ballad singer whose heavy drinking made him unable to provide his family with many of the bare necessities of life. Hannah Chaplin, to help with the financial difficulties, did needlework in the evenings after singing, dancing, and playing the piano during the day. The infant and his four-year-old half-brother Sydney (Hannah had been married twice before) survived as best they could the hectic life of theatrical people, always traveling from one town to another, living in cheap rooms, and eating whatever and whenever they could.

Shortly after Charles' first birthday, his mother and father separated, and the fragile, sensitive woman became the children's sole support. It proved too much for her. The long hours and the constant pressure affected her singing voice and abruptly ended Hannah's stage career. She also began getting severe headaches which caused her to fail at every job she undertook. Gradually the desperate family began to sink further and further into the London slums, where the undersized Charlie quickly learned to use his wit and speed against the street bullies and thieves. Rarely were the three Chaplins at peace and often they were hungry and without shelter.

After four years of utter poverty, Hannah could endure the hardships no more. She took herself and the two boys to the Lambeth Workhouse and put the family at the mercy of the county officials. There she knew they would get at least food and shelter.

Within three weeks, Charles and Syd were moved to the Hanwell schools, a dismal and vicious institution for orphans and penniless people who sadly discovered what it meant to rely on someone else's mercy. During the next eighteen months, Chaplin suffered many cruel punishments at the hands of the inhuman authorities who were determined to make the students obey and conform to the school's harsh rules. To add to his troubles, he was separated, when he was six, from Sydney, who was given brief training in the Navy. By the time he was seven, the lonely and friendless little boy had developed a stubbornness and a determination to do things his way, whatever the consequences.

About this time, Hannah tried to start a new life outside the poor house for the family, but the precious freedom was short-lived and the three of them were once more left at the hands of workhouse officials. It was during this second confinement that Chaplin's mother went insane and had to be committed to an asylum.

The legal authorities now ordered that Charlie's father assume custody of the two boys, and for the first and only time, the youngster got to know his father. What he saw of the man's drunkenness and brawling left such a psychological scar on him that for most of his early life Chaplin refused to drink any form of alcohol.

His brief stay with his father ended when Hannah, once more recovered, was again able to support her children. By then both boys had had a number of contacts with the stage and decided that a theatrical career was the best way to rise above their pitiful state. After various odd jobs, Charles, not yet nine years old, landed a part with a traveling dance act called "The Eight Lancashire Lads."

It was while he was traveling with this group of preteenagers that Chaplin became fascinated with acrobatics and pantomime. Since every boy wanted to do a "solo" number, each began working up his own special routine. Charles discovered that nothing better bridged the gap between himself and the rough, brawling audiences in the mining camps than some good mimicking and acrobatic tricks. To improve his skill, the alert youngster studied and practiced everyone else's act. By the time he left the troupe a year and a half later, Chaplin had started to master many of the basics of stagecraft.

When the youngster came back to Hannah and Syd, he found life as difficult as ever. To help, the older brother decided to work on a passenger boat. This not only gave the mother one son less to take care of, but also provided her with some added income. Now, for a short period, Chaplin and his mother had time alone with each other. She became his friend and his teacher, and to pass away the lonely hours, the two of them took turns mimicking their neighbors and the people who passed outside their window. Not only did Hannah teach him some valuable lessons in pantomime, but more important, she impressed the twelve-year-old boy with the pleasure poor people got in pretending that they were better off than it seemed, and certainly far superior to those they imitated.

But Chaplin was not to know happiness for very long. During his brother's second voyage, Hannah again lost her reason and had to be recommitted to a sanitarium. This became the pattern for the rest of her life. Months passed before Sydney returned, and Charles, alone (his father had died two years before), lived as a vagabond in the London streets, begging his food, sleeping in the gutters, and matching his wits against prostitutes, drunkards, and gang-lords.

Finally Syd came back, discovered his brother's sad predicament and took matters in hand. Now all their energies were spent in developing their talents as actors. Long into the evenings they practiced their dancing, singing, acrobatics, and pantomime.

By 1905, Charles was so well on with his skill that he got the key part of Billy, the messenger boy, in *Sherlock Holmes,* a popular stage play. Legend has it that one night backstage in a London theater the sixteen-year-old actor met the famous creator of the great fictional detective, and Sir Arthur Conan Doyle jokingly made a pact with Chaplin that they would ever after split their earnings.

In the meantime, Sydney joined the Fred Karno pantomime company, one of the most important comedy groups at the turn of the century. Karno, a former acrobat whose real name was Fred Wescott, had by the early 1900's perfected a marvelous new form of pantomime, "a wordless play," where talented actors, highly skilled in split-second timing, burlesque, and acrobatics, delighted audiences with their slapstick sketches about the madcap antics of drunks, tramps, thieves, boxers, magicians, and policemen.

Soon after Charles finished his engagement with the "Sherlock Holmes" company, Syd managed to get him a job with Karno. This was his big break. In one bit part after another, the clever and hard-working Chaplin perfected his pacing, mimicking, tumbling, dancing, and gag routines. After work, he kept to himself, content to eat his three meals a day and put most of his money in the bank.

It was during this period in his life that Charles met and fell in love with the sister of one of Karno's actors. But he always considered Hetty Kelly too good for him and took pleasure in just watching her from afar. For months, the pathetic little teenager followed Hetty around, inventing excuses just to be near her or finding out where she was going so he could trail her at a distance. At other times, he sat on lonely park benches thinking about the beautiful but unattainable Hetty. She never knew of his deep love, nor did anything ever happen in those days to change their relationship. But she remained in his mind for the rest of his professional life.

Since Karno's troupe was really a group of companies, traveling anywhere for money and comedy, Charles got a chance to tour on the continent and the United States. His specialty became imitating a "drunken" gentleman who interferes with actors doing their song-and-dance routines. In England the sketch was known as "Mumming Birds," but in America it was called "A Night in an English Music Hall."

It was while Chaplin was on his second tour to the United States in April, 1913, that Sennett and Normand caught his act and decided to bring him to Hollywood.

The Chaplin legend began almost from the moment the Keystone boss saw the thin, small, twenty-four-year-old actor without his stage make-up and costume. The shocked Sennett was sure Kessel had hired the wrong comic. Charles, both to hide his insecurity and to convince Mack that there was no mistake, put on a little comedy show to display his worth. Nevertheless, Sennett remained uneasy. After a brief and awkward conversation, Chaplin was told to report for work the next day.

It took three days, however, for the worried young man to return to Keystone. The first two times Chaplin came as far as the front gate and then, scared to enter, he quickly returned to his cheap hotel room opposite a theater. (He had chosen this particular hotel because the only person Chaplin knew in town was the stage doorman who worked across the street.) Only after Sennett made a personal telephone call to find out what was wrong did the little fellow appear at the Edendale Studio.

In December, 1913, there weren't many film people friendly to stage actors. It hadn't been long before that stage actors had considered movie roles beneath their dignity. Now the screen actors, flush with their rising popularity, snubbed their noses at the "amateur" theatrical players who were "just breaking" into the art of the film.

The Keystone troupe shared these feelings about theatrical people and let the inexperienced Chaplin know it. For almost two weeks, he sat by, ignored, apparently in the way, and watched and studied the hectic pace of slapstick film making. In the meantime, everyone made wisecracks about the unsociable "Limey" who had "swindled" Sennett.

Finally, Chaplin got his first chance to act in movies. The film was called "Making a Living," and Charles played the part of a cad who uses his friendship with a society girl to get some "shocking" pictures and sell them to a newspaper. Unfortunately for Chaplin, Henry Lehrman was the film's director, and he intended to set the newcomer straight on just how things were done at Keystone. While Charles admitted he knew nothing about film making, he argued that he knew a great deal about comedy. And during the three days it took to make the movie, Chaplin and Lehrman constantly fought. The film director pointed out that cutting and gags counted more than stage routines, while the stubborn actor pleaded for more time to develop his characterization.

Word was sent to Sennett that his new performer was a troublemaker, a know-it-all who was going to cost the studio a fortune because he took too much time getting into the swing of things. This resulted in twice as much film being used as normally required. So the boss came down from his tower and gave Chaplin a scolding in front of the crew. As he had done all his life, the young man listened politely, never answered back, and then continued to do just what he felt like.

After the film was finished, Lehrman, unknown to Chaplin, worked with the editor to mis-cut any of the actor's scenes that appeared funny. Thus, when "Making a Living" was shown, it was a flop and not many people thought Charles was any good, even the actor himself.

Less than forty-eight hours after his first film was finished, Chaplin, in street clothes, was idly watching Sennett direct a hotel lobby scene for Normand's next movie called "Mabel's Strange Predicament." To give the action some more humor, Mack began looking for ways to add gags to the plot when all of a sudden he spied Charles. He shouted to him to get into some funny outfit and do some comedy routines before the camera. Legend has it that on the way to the wardrobe to get a costume, Chaplin decided to dress-up as a seedy dandy, somewhat in the style of what Max Linder did in France. Since he shared a dressing room with Arbuckle and other comics, he knew that they would have what he needed. From Roscoe, he borrowed a baggy pair of pants. From Ford Sterling he took old and oversized shoes. And because he knew that Sennett considered him rather young-looking, Chaplin penciled in a thin moustache to make himself appear older. On the way back to the set he picked up a small derby hat, a cane, and a tight little coat. And then in true music-hall tradition, he began to strut on stage, awkward, foolish, and incredibly funny. For almost ten minutes he kept everyone doubled over with laughter and the seed for the immortal "Charlie the film tramp" was planted. Nine years later, when the character was not only fully developed but widely imitated, Chaplin would explain that his costume symbolized the comedian's understanding of the average man: "The derby (bowler), too small, is striving for dignity. The mustache is vanity. The tightly buttoned coat and the stick and his whole manner are a gesture towards gallantry and dash and 'front.' He is trying to meet the world bravely, to put up a bluff, and he knows that, too. He knows it so well that he can laugh at himself, and pity himself a little."

In this second film, Chaplin was far from being aware of the great possibilities that the tramp personality had for him. And so were the people of Keystone. One funny scene hardly made for a great career. Months passed before the film apprentice became accepted as an equal, let alone a star. In the meantime, the young man from poverty row worked day and night to learn the secrets of film comedy. He made friends with the key comics, spent long hours with Mabel Normand discussing screen technique, and watched the various directors at work.

Always the challenge before him was in how to merge his music-hall experience into the manufactured madness of the Keystone formula. Each film part required him to act aggressively in a broad, farcical style. But he always tried to hold back on the mugging, take more time with character development, show more imagination in the kinds of comic possibilities. Only Chaplin's belief in himself kept him going in the first part of 1914. Rumors circulated around the studio that Sennett was about to give him some cash and send the brash entertainer back to England.

Then one day all that changed. Legend has it that Kessel wired Mack to keep the Chaplin comedies coming. Exhibitors and audiences alike were wild about him. So Sennett, being a greedy businessman, began to let Chaplin write and direct his own films; this made the new film genius more sure than ever that he knew what was best for him. Maybe Keystone pictures were not suitable for his great pantomime, but they offered him a chance to test his Karno routines on the screen. Of the thirty-five movies he made for Sennett, the star directed twenty-two. And in these early attempts, you begin to see his inventive mind playing with inanimate objects and the gags that result when windows, doors, and stage props confuse the little fellow. It was as if Chaplin owned a dictionary of comic ideas.

Of course, Sennett rewarded the productive comic with a $25 raise, and Chaplin, in turn, confided to his boss that as soon as he made his first $100,000, he was getting out of this crazy "racket." He also asked his employer to hire Sydney, returning his brother's favor with Karno, and by mid-1914 the two Chaplins were once more working together.

Sennett was also in the mood for returning favors. It all came about because Griffith was getting a lot of publicity out of his forthcoming feature film, eventually called *The Birth of a Nation,* and the Keystone director was jealous. So Mack decided to direct the first full-length comedy movie. The picture was named *Tillie's Punctured Romance* and told the story about a city slicker (Chaplin) who, together with his girl friend (Normand) took advantage of Tillie, the farmer's daughter. To play the part of Tillie, Sennett hired Marie Dressler, the actress who twelve years before had written the letter to Belasco. This was her first film, and although she did not do much in the silent era of film, in the Thirties she became one of Hollywood's greatest comediennes, winning an Academy Award in 1931 for clowning in *Min and Bill,* also starring another Sennett discovery, Wallace Beery!

After *Tillie's Punctured Romance* (which took fourteen weeks to make), everyone knew about the great Chaplin and all the major studios tried to get him away from Keystone. As a defensive measure, Sennett gave strict orders that no one was allowed near the popular star. In the meantime, the two men began negotiations for a new contract. Sennett offered him $400 a week. Chaplin asked for $750. But neither one seriously considered the present relationship acceptable. Keystone had its basic way of making a comedy film, and the little comic wanted more freedom to experiment.

Thus it came as no surprise when in January, 1915, the star signed with Broncho Billy's company, Essanay. What was unusual was Chaplin's $1,250-a-week salary, almost ten times what he had made the year before and an indication of what was to follow.

At Essanay, in the fourteen films Chaplin made between February, 1915, and April, 1916, the remarkable entertainer began to refine his basic formula for most of his future comedies. He knew the worth of the Keystone organization, with its marvelous array of talent and its emphasis on comic improvisation. But he also knew, without the help of any formal education in classic humor, that great comedy contained some precious wisdom that made it possible for the average man, through laughter, to endure disappointment and defeat. His past had taught him how mime and humor also could act as the individual's safe rebellion against poverty and humiliation. What was needed now was some character, some special makeup with which the audience could relate to him, and with which he might be able to symbolize the poor man's eternal struggle against hunger and loneliness. And slowly, surely, from the depths of his experience, the tramp idea began to take shape. Through the role of the seedy little vagabond, Chaplin fashioned a visual symbol for which people, in general, felt a comradeship. When "the little fellow" loves and loses, when he refuses to surrender to power and poverty, when he confuses and confounds the forces that by all standards of reason and logic should destroy him, Chaplin became the favorite star of millions. To put it another way, the tramp who could kick up his heels and try again gave film audiences the kind of happy propaganda they were after.

He also gave them a unique kind of comedy hero, one who brought a touch of pathos as well as laughter. Always we were to be reminded that rebellion is not without a price tag, that in the end the only weapon against defeat is the hope that tomorrow things might be better.

It was during his Essanay period that Chaplin met a lovely blonde secretary who fitted perfectly his idea of a screen heroine. So he convinced Edna Purviance to become his leading lady and for the next nine years she became the reason that "the tramp" strove for nobility and success. Although they were inseparable on the screen, Charles and Edna maintained separate private lives. No matter how many fabulous offers she got to leave her benefactor, she worked only for him until her retirement in 1923. In gratitude, Chaplin kept her on his payroll until she died in 1958.

Ben Turpin also got his start with Chaplin at Essanay, but the two were never able to establish a good working relationship. In Chaplin's life, there was room for only one star, so Ben left for Keystone and made his own kind of film history.

Although Chaplin by now was an international star, his work still needed improvement. Many of his plots were weak and contrived, and except for the master clown's superb timing and excellent pantomime, the films seemed senseless. He needed more time to perfect his narrative technique. Then, as he started to rely more and more on his personal experiences to guide him in his work, it became impossible for Chaplin to remain at Essanay. The studio heads tried to discourage him (by now an impossible task) from getting so serious in his movies. The eternal struggle between art and business forced him to find a company that would allow him to make films his way.

Legend has it that the great comedian had no idea just how famous he was at the start of 1916. Syd, who had arranged for a new contract, wired him to come to New York to sign with Mutual. Chaplin got on a train and headed East. At every major stop along the way, thousands of people gathered, just to catch a glimpse of the brilliant comic. When he finally reached New York, Chaplin knew his worth. On February 26, 1916, he agreed to work for the Mutual Film Corporation, to make twelve films in seventeen months at . . . $10,000 a week, plus a $150,000 bonus just for signing. Before the train trip, he would have happily settled for a quarter of that deal.

It was during his Mutual period that Chaplin perfected his tramp formula, mixing laughter and tears into magnificent comedy. Beginning in May, 1916, with *The Floorwalker* and following with such heralded minor masterpieces as *The Vagabond, The Pawnshop, Behind the Screen, The Rink, Easy Street, The Immigrant,* and *The Adventurer,* the immortal clown mastered the skill of screen gags, suitable plots, and effective characterizations.

Now for the first time, the tramp represented more than just one group or nation. He stood for "Everyman" in search of love and dignity, and he challenged the rich and the powerful who had abused their authority to humiliate others. It was the start of Chaplin's crusade against the evils he had known at close range and the attempt to reform society through his comic genius.

In the months that followed, he became more deeply involved in his comedies than ever before. To perfect his social criticism, Chaplin took more time with each movie, rehearsing instead of improvising, carefully planning each gag so that it squeezed every laugh out of a comic routine.

Soon audiences came to expect great things from "Charlie the tramp" and they were not disappointed. No matter what problems the little fellow faced, he remained proud and boastful. His outward appearance lied; he was a true gentleman whose sense of humanity made him a champion of the cause of justice. And he enjoyed a good joke now and then. What was most wonderful about him, he dismissed the world as it was and made it over as he wanted it to be.

In his fantasy world, Chaplin needed a giant actor against whom he could contrast effectively his size and agility. Eric

Campbell fitted the part perfectly. The forty-six-year-old Scots-
man was a marvelous villain, and in the eleven films they did
together, he gave the tramp every opportunity to use his speed
and wit to defeat the awesome "Goliath." Less than two years
after he first appeared with Chaplin in *The Floorwalker,*
Campbell, a gentle man in real life, was tragically killed in an
automobile accident.

There is little doubt that Chaplin enjoyed himself most
fulfilling his Mutual contract. He was single, fast becoming a
millionaire, and the most sought-after celebrity in the world.
His success seemed even more spectacular when he left Mutual
in mid-1917 and joined First National to make eight two-reel
comedies for the huge sum of $1,200,000. This new-found
wealth, plus his savings, gave him the chance to build his
own studio where the star could make films the way he desired.
At twenty-seven years of age, he appeared to be the luckiest
man alive.

But appearances were deceiving. Success was beginning to
exact its toll from him. At first the attacks on Chaplin centered
on what many people felt to be distasteful and vulgar bits in his
pictures. Then came the resentment among exhibitors who felt
they had to pay too high a price to rent his films. To irritate
them even more, distributors had started block-booking prac-
tices, which forced the theater owners to rent a lot of bad movies in order to get one Chaplin film. Next came the abusive attacks on the British actor for not serving in the English army
during World War I. Even though he tried to enlist several times
and was rejected, the public, for months during 1917, criticized
him unjustly and harshly. Few of his critics took note of the
millions of dollars in savings bonds that Chaplin, along with
Mary Pickford, Douglas Fairbanks, and William S. Hart raised

for the war effort. (The friendship among these performers resulted the following year in the birth of United Artists. At the last minute Hart refused to join because he didn't want to spend his own money, and thus missed the chance of a lifetime. Griffith became the fourth partner.)

But all these problems were minor compared to the personal ones starting in 1918. Chaplin had met and become romantically involved with sixteen-year-old Mildred Harris. It has never been uncommon for starlets to pursue big stars in hopes of furthering their careers, nor is it unusual for the stars to use their positions to attract beautiful bedfellows. The unfortunate thing here was that Miss Harris, pretending she was pregnant, forced Chaplin to marry her on October 23, 1918. More than a thirteen-year age difference separated the ill-matched couple. The wife was a young, flighty, and stage-struck girl, while the husband was a mature, moody, and frugal man. Nevertheless, the couple tried to make a go of the marriage, but when their malformed son was born in the summer of 1919 and died three days later, Chaplin decided to leave Mildred. That fall they separated and before the end of the year ugly and vicious stories about their personal and private lives appeared in the press. It took almost twelve months to get the divorce case settled, and in the meantime the image of the happy-go-lucky tramp was getting smeared.

Four years later Chaplin again married a sixteen-year-old girl whose stage name was Lita Grey. Once more history and the movie world repeated themselves. The incompatible couple had two children before the inevitable break-up occurred. Only now, the wife had a clever mother who was not about to let the husband get away without proper support. Chaplin refused the alimony figure, and the case went to court. For six months, scandal mongers dragged the helpless comic through the head-lines and by the time the divorce was granted on August 22, 1927, the famous actor appeared to many as a vicious and self-ish man whose lustful desires for young girls made him unfit both as a husband and father.

The charges were repeated in the years to come with false paternity suits and smutty rumors. Looking back on the facts of all the divorce cases and charges, we see that Chaplin was no-where near the villain he was pictured. It seems now as if a fickle public was jealous of a poor boy who had made good.

While Chaplin's personal problems increased in 1917, so did his artistic greatness. In films like *A Dog's Life* and *Shoul-der Arms* (both released in 1918), *The Kid* (1921, in which Chaplin made Jackie Coogan a star), and *The Pilgrim* (1923, his last film for First National), the great mime-actor had turned away from his brilliant two-reelers and put himself on the threshold of his great feature-length films.

In the meantime, the cinema's golden age of comedy was at hand. A number of unusual men had left the stage to chal-lenge Chaplin's and Sennett's fame and fortune. Foremost among the newcomers was a vaudevillian acrobat, who in 1917, after one day's shooting, decided that come what may, he was going to work in films.

Charles Spencer Chaplin, one of the greatest artists of the twentieth century.

Chaplin began his movie career in this film, "Making a Living" (1914), as a shifty and nasty character.

Chaplain became an overnight sensation in this first feature film
is the irate wife who is being fooled by

comedy called "Tillie's Punctured Romance" (1914). Marie Dressler
her husband (Chaplin) and the maid (Normand).

By the time he made this second Mutual film, "The Fireman" (1916), Charlie had perfected much of his film image. His leading lady is Edna Purviance.

His next film, "The Vagabond" (1916), saw Chaplin developing his gift for pathos and comedy in the picture of the little tramp.

The idea of the little fellow and his girl triumphing against
giant villains proved very successful in this scene from Chaplin's
seventh Mutual masterpiece, "Behind the Screen" (1916).
Purviance plays the sweetheart and Eric Campbell the trapped
villain.

The universal appeal of Charlie the downtrodden was solidified in this scene from "The Immigrant" (1917) when Chaplin, comforting a lonely girl (Purviance) and her mother, views the Statue of Liberty for the first time.

Considered to be one of the most publicized stills in all film history, this shot shows Charlie as the tramp who befriends a small boy (Jackie Coogan) in "The Kid" (1921). This was Chaplin's first full-length comedy that he wrote, directed, and starred in. It also made Coogan the greatest child star of his day.

Lita Grey, who played one of the children in a dream scene in "The Kid," became Chaplin's second wife. They are shown here with Charles, Jr., prior to their sensational divorce trial.

One of the most historic moments in screen history is shown here
Artists Corporation on April 17, 1919. Left to right in the
Charles Chaplin, and Douglas Fairbanks, Sr.

when the papers of incorporation were signed creating United
foreground are the founders, D. W. Griffith, Mary Pickford,
In the background are their attorneys.

The Human Mop
BUSTER KEATON

One cold day in March, 1917, Lou Anger, the manager of Joseph M. Schenck Film Enterprises, was on his way up Broadway to check on the company's new producing unit just created for Roscoe "Fatty" Arbuckle, who, after four years with Sennett, now wanted to make his own movies. By accident, Lou met the son of an old vaudeville friend and invited the twenty-one-year-old stage comic to meet Arbuckle and watch the making of a film comedy called "The Butcher Boy." Since he had nothing better to do, the young man, who was ignorant about movies, agreed to go to the studio, an old converted warehouse, a few blocks away.

73

Arbuckle instantly developed a fondness for the comic whose name was Keaton, and the two spent the day and most of the night creating sight gags for the new two-reeler. Early the next morning, Keaton informed his agent that he was breaking his musical comedy contract and going to work for Arbuckle. When the agent asked him about his new salary, Buster had to admit that he hadn't actually been offered a job, and it wasn't until after a few day's work that he discovered he was making $40 a week.

In the ten years that followed, Buster Keaton, with his great stone face, developed the famous screen image of the rejected young lover who tries to prove his worth by bravely fighting against stupid people, giant machines, and the titanic forces of nature itself. Children and grown-ups flocked to his films, and after 1920, intellectuals began to praise him as one of the cinema's immortals. In 1949, James Agee, in his famous essay for *Life* magazine entitled "Comedy's Greatest Era," pointed out, "No other comedian could do as much [as Keaton could] with the dead pan. He used this great, sad, motionless face to suggest various related things: how dead a human being can get and still be alive; or, an awe-inspiring sort of patience and power to endure, proper to granite but uncanny in the form of flesh and blood. Everything he was and did bore out this rigid face and played laughs against it. When he moved his eyes, it was like seeing them move in a statute." At the Venice Film Festival in 1965, almost forty years since his last major film, great directors like Fellini, Godard, Visconti, and Antonioni were ignored by thousands of young people to give Keaton a five-minute standing ovation. And in 1970, two years after the famous comedian's death, a Keaton film revival started in New York City. Andrew Sarris, noted movie critic for *The Village Voice,* wrote at the time, "Keaton can be very funny on occasion, but he can also show sadness, love, despair, resignation, absorption, abstraction, cruelty, and compassion. He can be a satirist, a mimic, a character, a caricature. Of all the artists who have ever worked in the movies, Keaton and Hitchcock strike me as the two who were unblocked by something magical in the medium itself. Their greatness is not in themselves but in their marriage to the motion of pictures."

Although he began and ended his life with applause, Buster Keaton's story is filled with years of sadness and misfortunes.

He was born Joseph Francis Keaton on October 4, 1895, to theatrical gypsies who made their living performing in traveling medicine shows. His father, Joseph Hallie Keaton (hereafter to be called Joe), did acrobatic tricks and dancing, while his wife, Myra, played a saxophone. At the time Francis arrived in the world, Joe's touring companion in show business was Harry Houdini (later to be known as the Great Houdini) who did a few card tricks before he thrilled audiences with his escapes from policeman's handcuffs. After the show, Harry sold "magic medicine" to the local yokels for a buck a bottle.

Six months after he was born, Francis crawled out of his crib and fell down a flight of steps, but was miraculously unhurt. Houdini, who reached the infant first, comforted the astonished parents by saying "That's some buster your baby took." The name "Buster" suited Francis and from then on he became known as Buster Keaton.

Soon after that, Houdini left the company, starting a quick climb toward fame and fortune. Joe, envious of his friend's success, suddenly decided to give up his medicine-show life.

What gave him such confidence was Buster's addition to the act, now called "The Three Keatons." Joe had discovered that his kid was a natural tumbler and acrobat. No matter what the father did to his son—throw, hit, or drop him—Buster never cried and rarely got hurt. Soon the two of them had worked out a special routine. The three-year-old, in full view of the audience, began by annoying his parent, who in turn tossed the mischievous kid all around the stage and ended by sliding him across the floor, as if he were a "human mop." At first, Buster showed the public how much he enjoyed Joe's roughhousing, but soon the intuitive performer realized that he got more laughs and applause by pretending indifference to all the violence. By the time he was five, Keaton not only had learned a great deal about stage acrobatics and comic routines, but he had also become the star of the act.

Thus "The Three Keatons" came to Broadway.

They landed a job with Huber's Museum, an outgrowth of the famous institution owned by P. T. Barnum. In those days, museum entertainment featured two floors of entertainment. On the top floor, the Curio Hall, exhibitors exploited deformed and unfortunate freaks as curiosities for a thrill-seeking public, while on the main floor there was a fifty-minute variety show, with an emphasis on soft-shoe dancing and acrobatics. "The Three Keatons" were billed to appear on the ground floor.

In the seventeen years the trio stayed together, it was considered one of the roughest acts in show business. Sometimes this reputation helped the family. It brought them lots of publicity, and with publicity came better bookings, good spots on the bill, and respectable salaries. But the publicity also brought the Gerry Society after Joe Keaton.

At the turn of the century social reformers had finally

managed to stop many of the injustices that the Industrial Revolution had instituted against children, particularly in terms of work and welfare. The Gerry Society was one Eastern group that watched show business to see that children weren't mistreated in the theater. They immediately got after Pappa Keaton and kept Buster from appearing at Huber's.

It was about then that the six-year-old spent his one and only day in public school. At another actor's suggestion, Myra had enrolled Buster in a New Jersey school close to the theater the family was playing. At precisely 8 A.M. the boy was in the principal's office and within an hour had been assigned to a first grade teacher. When the teacher took attendance, he made wisecracks just the way he did in the act. When she taught the geography lesson, he ad-libbed. By the time Buster had destroyed the grammar session, the frustrated school marm had had enough. She marched him to the principal who, in turn, expelled the fresh kid and sent home a note to the amused parents pleading with them never to send Buster back. So Mamma Keaton became his teacher.

In the meantime, the Gerry Society continued to hound the trio, claiming the child's age and the family's act violated the Child Labor Laws. Finally in December, 1907, they obtained a court order against Joe which forbade "The Three Keatons" to perform in New York for two years, until Buster was sixteen. (No one knew the boy's exact age. In 1909, he was only fourteen.)

But the reformers were only one-half of Joe's troubles in 1907. The other half was the United Booking Office, the major source of jobs for vaudevillians. Ever since Tony Pastor had cleaned up vaudeville, a group of theater owners, headed by B. F. Keith and Edward F. Albee, had tried to take over the industry. The exhibitors shrewdly discovered that by owning the theaters they could control not only the bookings but also the actor's wages and thus make tremendous profits at the performers' expense. The theory went into practice in the form of the United Booking Office, which discriminated against actors whom Keith and Albee didn't like. The best jobs came from the UBO and naturally the actors hated the unfair conditions; therefore minor revolutions occurred from time to time. Each time Joe sided with the reformers, and each time Keith and Albee won, making it harder and harder for "The Three Keatons" to get good working arrangements. In 1907, Joe had sided with the Shubert exhibitors against the UBO and both had lost the fight after three months.

Thus with New York closed to them as well as the UBO out for revenge, the Keatons went to England to perform. But there too they found trouble. This time it was the audience who didn't like the act's violence. Many people thought that Buster was Joe's adopted son and that the father didn't like him very much. Although Joe toned down the roughhousing in the days that followed, he made up his mind to go back to America and after a week's work in London, they were on their way home.

These events started Joe's days of heavy drinking and constant despair. And these in turn affected the act. Keep in mind that each time the Keatons appeared on stage they improvised their routines. It was never done the same way twice in a row. When Joe was "right," the two fellows had a lot of fun inventing new bits of business and surprising each other. But when Joe was "out of sorts," everyone's timing was off and no one was safe on stage. The key to their act, like most vaudeville acts, was discipline and organization. Underlying each performance was a basic pattern suggesting a starting point that progressed methodically to its conclusion. Although the violence might appear in new forms each night, the Keatons structured their gags to fit into a situation that became funnier and funnier as the comics proceeded. But when Joe didn't have control of himself, he couldn't control the pace and timing of the violence or the progress of the act. Thus it became more and more dangerous for Buster to appear on stage.

It was about this time that the teenager began developing a number of interests that stayed with him throughout his life. Baseball became one of his favorite pastimes and in his years in Hollywood, Buster not only had the best film hardball team but also arranged his movie contracts so that he could attend the World Series each year. The youngster also developed a life-long fascination for mechanical gadgets, spending countless hours experimenting with "Rube Goldberg bits"—intricate machines to perform simple acts. These mechanical gadgets later became crucial sight gags in his great movies. In *The Navigator* (1924), for example, Rollo (Keaton), the rich playboy, adrift at sea with his true love, creates a monstrous kitchen machine to make a simple breakfast. Everywhere you look, an intricate system of levers and pulleys and cords provide the two with coffee, eggs, and toast.

With the start of World War I in Europe, many foreign acts rushed to the safety of the United States, and the UBO, out to punish American performers who caused them trouble, gave immediate bookings to Europeans while acts like "The Three Keatons" got put on waiting lists. At this point in history, Martin Beck was the key figure of UBO, and Joe made it known wherever he played that Beck was a no-good dirty bum.

The feud came to a head in 1915 at the Palace where during their act on stage, Joe spied Beck in the wings. Legend has it that the UBO manager shouted to Joe, "Make me laugh, Keaton," and the incensed actor ran off stage, set to kill Beck.

Luckily for both men, the stagehands grabbed Joe while Beck ran madly into the street, fleeing for his life. But that incident, for all practical purposes, put an end to "The Three Keatons." Beck banned them from big-time vaudeville.

For the next year or so they played the small out-of-town vaudeville circuits but Joe's increased drinking plus the fact that the act now had to perform three shows a day instead of two ruined their timing and destroyed Buster's patience to endure the painful roughhousing.

Finally in February, 1917, Myra and Buster took their things and deserted Joe in San Francisco. She went to Detroit where the family had many friends, while the young actor journeyed to Broadway to begin his stage career as a solo performer. Since New York vaudeville was closed to him, he landed a job in musical comedy with the Schuberts, who ten years before had tried to fight the UBO. Two days prior to starting rehearsals, Buster met Lou Anger and went into movies.

In 1917, before the birth of giant studio control, the movie moguls left the making of comedy films to the comics themselves. Arbuckle's two-reelers were typical of the casual process by which cameramen and electricians were as much involved in creating the sight-gags and storyline as the performers were in constructing sets and arranging various camera angles and lighting effects. Roscoe not only starred in the pictures but he directed them as well. Furthermore, the fact that the crew acted as a team cut down on the cost and time required to make a movie and, as a result, Arbuckle turned out a successful comedy short every six weeks.

What was significant for Keaton in the fifteen shorts he made with Arbuckle was the similarity he discovered between the movies and vaudeville. He realized that the basic comedy precedents had been set by the stage and that he had to devise some method by which his love for realistic and logical comedy could fit into the flexible and fantastic world of film.

In addition to his valuable association with Arbuckle, Keaton met and formed a significant friendship with producer Joe Schenck. By 1918, Schenck realized that Keaton had the makings of a great star and intended to profit by Buster's talent. Besides, Keaton was becoming romantically involved with Joe's sister-in-law, Natalie.

Before anything could come of Schenck's discovery, Buster was drafted into the infantry and spent most of 1918 and the early part of 1919 in France.

When he returned to Hollywood, where the Schencks had moved the previous year, Keaton found the movie empire undergoing tremendous changes. The war had increased employment and more jobs meant more money for entertainment. This increased box-office wealth had made the exhibitors hungry for more power, and in 1919, men like Marcus Loew, Adolph Zukor, the Warner Brothers, and William Fox started to monopolize the motion picture industry much the way that Keith and Albee had taken over vaudeville. The powerful exhibitors rushed greedily to gobble up large theater chains while at the same time they bought film-producing companies to protect themselves against being left without enough movies at reasonable rentals for their theaters.

Joe Schenck, well aware of the new era just beginning, convinced Buster to let him star Buster in his own comedy shorts to be released through Metro pictures, an outfit soon to be purchased by his old friend Loew and managed by his brother Nick. Keaton agreed to the deal for several basic reasons. First, he trusted Joe. He had no reason not to. Second, Buster never really cared about financial matters. All his life he considered art more important than money and here was his chance to make movies his way and that's what he wanted to do. Third, Keaton was a fatalist. Ever since he was an infant, Buster had miraculously survived train wrecks, fires, and dangerous storms. He firmly believed that no matter what he did, fate would determine the outcome.

So the Keaton Film Corporation was formed, and Buster set about making motion picture history.

In the years from 1920 to1923, Keaton found life unbelievably blissful. Not only did he have complete freedom to make his own films, but his brand of comedy also proved to be very popular at the box-office.

The Keaton method stressed good acting in apparently logical situations which featured opportunities for daring feats and incredible sight gags. A good example was his short *One Week* made in 1920. A young bridegroom (Keaton) receives a "build-it-yourself" home for a wedding gift. Although the directions were simple, his wife's former boyfriend has changed the numbers on the various pieces. The hero begins to assemble his house on a Monday, but soon realizes something is wrong. Nevertheless, he refuses to be defeated by the machine-made package of parts. By Friday, the 13th, the Keaton character has constructed an insane but practical solution to his dilemma. Visitors to his house-warming party are shocked to see everything out of place, installed in strange ways, and near total collapse. To top things off, a sudden storm causes the house to spin like a carousel wheel, eventually throwing everyone out of the building.

The following day brings more trouble to the unhappy couple. Their "dream house" has been built on the wrong lot so it has to be moved. Buster gets the monstrosity as far as the local railroad tracks, but the house gets stuck on the rails. When one train just misses destroying it, the newlyweds think they are saved, and just at that moment another train arrives to smash the house into pieces. The unlucky couple walk off in search of better times.

Notable about *One Week* was the artist's visual style. His story had a beginning, middle, and end which depended upon film techniques, not words. The deadpan expression got him laughs because it suggested the comic's cool and restrained re-action to his problems, but it also signaled that he was devising some illogical but effective solution. Then when he swung into action, the contrast between the former static shot and the new dynamic motion proved humorous. So too did the contrast in visual size between the small figure of a man seen in a long shot next to a large building or mechanical thing. Keaton, more than any other of the great silent film comics, used the film's frame to show the difference between a man and a large object; the former small and stoical, the latter massive and monstrous. He also used the long shot to show how his hero by natural ac-robatic skill and split-second timing escaped dangerous situa-tions. By keeping his camera pulled back from the action, Kea-ton showed that his daring stunts were without the use of trick photography, stunt men, or special effects.

In the following two years, Keaton's series of two-reelers included such minor masterpieces as *Neighbors, Cops,* and *The Baloonatic.* With these he perfected his basic story formula that was to win him his great fame. The films featured a sceptical little fellow in love with a girl who asked that he prove himself before she became his wife. Indifferent to danger, the deter-mined hero faced greater and greater difficulties until in the end only superhuman inventiveness and superb athletic skill en-abled him to overcome the hostility of giant bullies, an entire police force, and nature itself.

By now Keaton rivaled the great Chaplin. Not only did

the critics feel he was as inventive, but also that he excelled the master clown in acrobatic agility. Buster, reflecting on the differences between Chaplin and himself, wrote in his autobiography *My Wonderful World of Slapstick,* "Charlie's tramp was a bum with a bum's philosophy. Lovable as he was, he would steal if he got the chance. My little fellow was a working man and honest."

But by 1923 changes were occurring in Hollywood that would tragically affect Keaton's life. Less than two years before, his close friend Arbuckle, after making three straight films without a day off, decided to drive up to San Francisco for a Labor Day weekend vacation. During a riotous party that lasted for three days, a minor bit-player became violently ill and blamed her condition on Roscoe's advances toward her. There was no truth to the charges and Arbuckle returned to Los Angeles the following Tuesday. That Friday she died and the next day the innocent star was accused of murder. A yellow press once more fed a hypocritical nation a series of lies about the sex-crazed Hollywood, and mass reform movements arose to boycott Arbuckle's films. Roscoe went through three trials, the first two resulted in hung juries, but the third time he was proven innocent of any crime and the judge declared that the nation owed the tragic star an apology. Few in the public cared about the facts and the man. America, in the midst of a wild depression, felt that the stars had it too good and they intended to make them pay for their wealth and status.

In the meantime, Joe Schenck had started releasing Buster's films through First National, and the bosses there decided that Keaton was making too much money for each short. (In 1922, he got $1,000 a week plus twenty-five percent of the net profits.) So they sent him a telegram claiming that his shorts were no longer worth the price and they weren't going to renew his contract. Actually, it was a bluff to make Buster feel insecure before the new contract talks began, but the idea backfired. Keaton got so angry that he refused to make any more movies for First National and demanded that Joe make new arrangements.

By now Keaton and Schenck were in-laws and things were not going well in the Keaton household. He had discovered to his horror that Natalie loved her family and money more than she did her husband. Joe, it seemed, sided more with his wife's folks than with his brother-in-law.

To make matters worse, Joe forced Buster into a deal with Metro pictures. It came about because in 1923 Loew was just about ready to consolidate all his holdings into a giant organization that was to become Metro-Goldwyn-Mayer.

Crucial to Keaton's career was the fact that Joe made a deal to help his brother Nick by bringing Keaton to M-G-M. At first Buster refused. Being friendly with Chaplin, he asked the great comic's advice, and Charles told him to go into business for himself. That way no one could tell Buster what to do. He explained that was why United Artists had been formed, to protect the stars from being exploited by the producers and exhibitors. But Keaton decided against the idea. He tried one last chance before he gave in and went to work for M-G-M.

Early in 1923, Buster went to see Adolph Zukor, head of Paramount Pictures. The great stone face comic explained that he wanted to change studios, but Zukor, regretfully couldn't hire him, for two reasons. First, he had been warned by Loew that Keaton was the property of M-G-M. Second, Zukor had just obtained the contract of a comic star who rivaled Chaplin and Keaton at their best.

The Three Keatons, the popular vaudeville act of

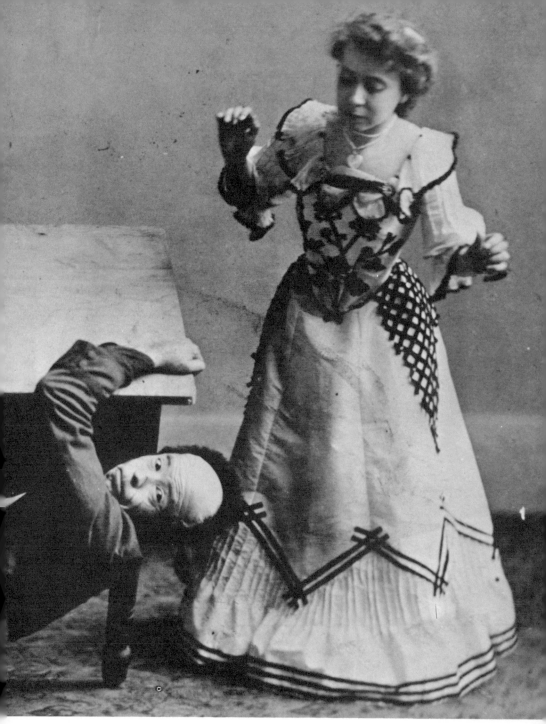

1900; from left to right: Buster, Joe, and Myra.

A typical Keaton gag was to have his hero concentrate on one thing while he was accidentally getting into greater problems.

Buster often claimed that his role as the weak little rich boy forced to turn prizefighter was one of his favorites. The movie was "Battling Butler" (1925).

Keaton's concern over the Arbuckle mess was reflected in this
trapped by fate into trouble with the police

1922 film classic "Cops." Buster is shown as an innocent man as he accidentally winds up in their parade.

By the early thirties, Keaton's mental health had weakened and it affected his appearance. Study Buster's face alongside those of the rising new film clowns from left to right: Oliver Hardy, Stan Laurel, and Jimmy Durante.

Keaton's last independent feature film was "Steamboat Bill, Jr." (1928), where he once more played a puny youngster who becomes a hero.

The Glass Comic
HAROLD LLOYD

In 1923 Adolph Zukor, Hollywood's most powerful producer, had just gone through three of his most difficult years in the film business. He had borrowed heavily to expand his theater holdings and then suddenly found himself in the midst of a tremendous censorship battle. Reformers, in particular, noted that most of the film capital's scandals involved Paramount employees: Arbuckle, Taylor, and Minter.

So Zukor began looking around for various ways to help improve his tainted screen image. At the same time, he was also looking for a fresh comic to replace Arbuckle, whom Will

Hays, the movie czar, had banned from the screen. Luckily for Zukor, there was a young man who needed a new distributor for his comedy films. Unlike Chaplin and Keaton, whose private lives by now had embarrassed their studios, Harold Lloyd's offstage career was a model of respectability. Everyone praised his sincerity, wholesomeness, and kindness. Even better for Zukor, Lloyd's money-making films emphasized normal people and clean humor. Consequently a meeting was arranged and in 1923 the all-American comic began releasing his movies through Paramount.

Harold Lloyd's amazing career reads as if it were written by a second-rate Hollywood producer. He was a poor boy who became a great and wealthy star, married his beautiful leading lady, and retired from the screen in the Thirties to live happily ever after. What's more, everyone loved him, and his famous competitors admired his style.

Keaton, for example, wrote in his autobiography, "Lloyd's screen character was quite different from both Chaplin's and mine. He played a mama's boy who continually surprised everyone, including himself, by triumphing over an impossible situation and displaying, in fits and starts, the fighting heart of a lion. Often Lloyd seemed more acrobat than comedian. But whatever he was on screen he always did a lot better than all right." James Agee in his 1949 essay went further, "If great comedy must involve something beyond laughter, Lloyd was not a great comedian. If plain laughter is any criterion . . . few people have equaled him, and nobody has ever beaten him."

How was it possible in the jazz age with its emphasis on luxury and sex that Lloyd became such a great success? And why had he chosen a screen character so different from the other great comics? The answers, like all those of the other clowns, were to be found in his background.

Harold Clayton, the younger of two sons of James and Sarah Lloyd, was born on April 20, 1893, in Burchard, Nebraska. His father was a poor man who invested his money in a cheap photography business and then for the next dozen years traveled with his family trying to eke out a living from the small towns of Nebraska and Colorado.

Harold spent a great deal of his youth in public schools, unlike the other great clowns. While they were learning how to survive in a tough world, Lloyd was being taught the basic virtues of Victorian self-respect: dependability, perseverance, initiative, self-control, thrift, and the belief that in the end justice triumphs. In later years these traits were to become the essence of his screen hero's character.

Interestingly, his first contact with movies came in 1903 from a traveling medicine show (much like the one the Keatons worked in). After the actors finished their magic tricks, they showed the audience the Edison Company's popular film called "The Great Train Robbery." The youngster was impressed, but his ambitions were for the stage, not the screen. Like many a poor kid, he felt the footlights offered him a chance to rise above his humble life.

"I was average," Lloyd wrote in his 1928 autobiography *An American Comedy,* "and typical of the time and place . . . assuming that the average boy before the war [World War I] was moderately poor, that his folks moved a great deal, and that he worked for his spending money at any job that was offered." But Harold felt he was exceptional as far as his single-minded ambition was concerned. "As far back as memory goes, and to the exclusion of all else, I was stage crazy. There is no accounting for its strength and persistence, for it began before I ever saw a play, and there were no actors, so far as we know, in either my father's or mother's family."

Gaylord, his brother, shared Harold's love for the stage and together the two boys put on special acts for the family. At other times, they hung around the stage doors of the various stock companies passing through and took a number of backstage jobs.

By 1906, Lloyd had developed into a serious drama student and was taking stock parts in plays on a regular basis. That year in Omaha he met and developed a strong friendship with a featured actor in show business named John Lane Conner. He had also by 1906 developed into quite a fighter. It seems as if the name "Harold" implied that its owner was a sissy, and the youngster constantly had to "correct" that false impression. In fact, Lloyd was so good with his fists that he was seriously considering the fight business instead of the stage. But his mother ordered him to forget boxing.

Then in 1911 luck changed Lloyd's life. His father, who had drifted from one job to the next, won a negligence case against a brewery and came into possession of three thousand dollars. The family agreed to leave the midwest, but Harold and his father disagreed about the direction. The father felt like trying his luck in New York or Nashville, but Harold had his heart set on going to San Diego where his friend Conner had just started a drama school. A flip of a coin settled the dispute and the son won, sending the family west.

For some unknown reason James Lloyd went into the pool hall and lunch counter business. Harold, who was enrolled in high school, helped his father at work and spent all his remaining hours acting in school and stock company plays.

A story goes that during one particular play in 1912, Harold found himself in trouble. The other actor on stage suddenly got a severe nose bleed and had to exit into the wings for medical help. To stall for time, Lloyd did an ad-lib comic monologue and was rather impressed with the amount of laughs he received. The next day he made a point of bragging to Conner, who directed the show, just how funny he was. The director-producer tore into him; not only had the young man done a bad job with his comic routine, but considering how long he had been acting it was surprising how little he knew about timing gags and spacing them far enough apart to squeeze the last drop out of each joke. The detailed criticism by a man he respected made such an impression on Lloyd that he remembered it till the end of his life and he made spacing and timing two of the key concepts in his comedy films.

It was also in 1912 that he got his first acting job in the movies. The old Edison Company had come to California to make some westerns, and since their producing unit was near Conner's dramatic school they used his students as extras. Lloyd got three dollars to play a semi-nude Yaqui Indian who raced across the screen.

By the spring of 1913, Lloyd's father had failed with his pool hall business and had journeyed to Los Angeles where he found work as a shoe salesman. When Harold was graduated from high school he followed his father's trail.

Since he needed money to live and the legitimate theater didn't have many good prospects that spring for young actors, Lloyd got in touch with the Edison Company to see if they still needed extras. They said they did, and he worked for them until July, earning just enough to eat. But by mid-summer the eastern company, having shot enough footage, packed up its equipment and headed home.

That left Lloyd in need of a new studio to earn his living. Eventually the determined twenty-year-old decided on Universal, where four companies were working at once. But it wasn't that easy to get into Universal. A big fence surrounded the blocks of barren land and a tough old gateman guarded the one entrance. If you didn't know anyone, he sent you to a casting window with several benches in front. Although most parts were given out early in the morning, the casting office kept the unknown extras sitting on the benches until the afternoon, just in case a director decided at the last minute he needed some more people. It cost the studio nothing to use this hiring policy.

After a few disappointing days, Harold noticed that many of the extras and actors with their makeup on passed by the gateman at noon to eat at a lunch counter across from the studio. So one noon hour the clever Lloyd put on some makeup and when the crew started back into the studio, he joined in. The gateman didn't even look up.

While it was too late to work that afternoon, he used his time to make friends with some of the extras who the next morning sneaked him in through a studio window, and thus Harold Lloyd started working regularly in movies.

In the days that followed he got friendly with many of the assistant directors who, in 1913, were doing most of the hiring. But far more significant for motion picture history, he met and became friendly with a "cowboy" who could ride but not act. The man's name was Hal Roach, soon to become Sennett's greatest competitor and in the early days of sound films, Hollywood's best comedy producer. But in the beginning Lloyd's career was tightly intertwined with Roach's.

Hal Roach was born in Elmira, New York, on January 14, 1892. His father was in the insurance business and his mother, to help with the family's meager income, ran a boarding house.

After dinner, it was a tradition in the Roach household for one member of the family or a boarder to tell a story, but the boy preferred his grandfather's tales to all the others. The elderly man had been a watchmaker in his youth and his precision work had made him blind by the time Hal was born. To hold the youngster's interest, Grandpa Roach dramatized his stories and added special sound effects with his corncob pipe. It was only later in life that Hal discovered that those unusual stories were based on classic novels. Everyone who sat at the old man's feet, however, loved the dramatic manner in which the stories were told. "I think," Roach recalls, "a little of that storytelling ability was passed on to me because ninety percent of the success I have had in pictures has come from my ability to create a dramatic or humorous situation which works in a picture just that way."

In 1909, Roach's father decided that it was time for his teenage son to explore the world before he settled down in Elmira working as an engineer for the Lehigh Valley Railroad. So Hal traveled to Seattle to visit his aunt, but once there he became interested in prospecting for gold in the Yukon and wound up in Alaska spending the winter working on a pack train.

When summer came, the homesick eighteen-year-old returned to Seattle and drove ice cream trucks. That job brought him to California and by the time he was nineteen he had become a freight superintendent for mule teams.

He moved to Los Angeles and felt very proud of his progress until one day he read an ad in the newspaper, "Wanted, men in western costume. Pay: a dollar, car fare and lunch. Be in front of the post office." Curious as to what it was all about, he put on a cowboy suit, applied for the job, was picked, and soon found himself at Tom Ince's Bison studio, later to become Universal Pictures.

The scene being shot took place in a gambling hall, and Roach's Yukon experience had taught him a great deal about roulette tables. The director sensed the kid's talent and asked him to work for Bison on a regular basis. The salary was five dollars a day. That doesn't seem like much now, but in 1912 laborers got paid ten cents an hour and a full day's work netted them a dollar. Roach accepted the film offer.

By the time he met Lloyd, Roach had decided that he preferred to write and direct films instead of act in them. Lloyd impressed him as a man with experience and talent. Also, the newcomer had finally become convinced that his future lay in comedy rather than in dramatic roles. Then chance once more took a part in their careers.

Universal hired a new assistant director who decreed that starting right away extras would get three dollars instead of five. At first the actors rebelled, but then began to reconsider. Lloyd and Roach refused to work for those wages and left.

Lloyd got a job with the Oz Film Company, a small-time movie outfit owned and operated by L. Frank Baum, the author of *The Wizard of Oz*.

Roach, in the interval, convinced the owner of a successful car agency to stake him to his own producing company. For his first film, the fledgling producer figured that one-reel kid comedies would be unique and profitable. He hired a couple of child actors and got Lloyd to play the chauffeur who drives the kids to the beach and becomes the butt of their practical jokes. The comedy was a disaster, and as a result, Roach hired another actor plus an actress to increase the appeal of the films. He also decided to raise Lloyd's pay to five dollars a day, telling him to make up some comic character that movie fans could laugh at.

For the next five one-reel comedies the two men experimented with battered top hats, a variety of mustaches, and heavily padded jackets. The comic character that finally emerged was named "Willie Work" and it didn't click. Nevertheless, Roach put together a package of eight one-reel comedies and a couple of two-reel dramas and sent them to New York to a distributing agency run by four brothers named Warner. They, in turn, peddled the prints to Pathé, who paid them some money that never got back to Roach. The Warner Brothers figured they needed the cash more than the west coast producer.

Lloyd was also doing some figuring. He felt he was entitled to ten dollars a day, the same as the dramatic star was being paid. So after he finished a one-reel film called *Just Nuts,* he asked Roach for a raise. Roach pleaded poverty, saying that he couldn't afford *two* expensive players. Lloyd quit, and Roach hired another comic. Three pictures later Roach ran out of money and creditors, gave up his production unit, and went to work for Essanay, where Chaplin was starring.

Within three weeks, Lloyd got a job at Keystone. Try as he might, he couldn't make the grade with Sennett, and at one point, Sterling advised him to give up comedy and try dramatic roles.

Once more luck came to the rescue. Although *Just Nuts* was a senseless comedy, Pathé liked it and offered to back Roach in a new producing company if he could come up with a series of such movies.

Each of his three "stars" had gone to work for other studios, and only Lloyd agreed to return to the fold . . . that is, at fifty dollars a week. Roach agreed, and now for the first time the two great giants of film began to work steadily together.

Roach had a unique way of making pictures in 1915. As he described it, "Monday morning I would bring the group in and say, '*You* make up as a cop, *you* make up as a garbageman, *you* make up as a pedestrian.' We'd go out in the park, and we'd start to do something. By that time, I'd have an idea of what the sets were going to be. By noon, I would tell the set man what I wanted, and he would go back to the studio to get them ready." No doubt you recognize its similarity to the Keystone formula.

While Roach imitated Sennett's film method, Lloyd decided to imitate Chaplin's film image in the form of a comic character named "Lonesome Luke." Lloyd figured the whole world was on a Chaplin craze, so why not take advantage of the master clown's appeal.

The actor's idea was to reverse the "tramp" outfit. While Charlie's clothes were too big for him, Luke wore tight clothes that looked as if he had outgrown them. Lloyd's father even went to a Los Angeles repair store to buy an old pair of size 12AA shoes to complete his son's hayseed role.

At first not many people liked the obvious imitation of Chaplin, but the growing demand for "Charlie the Tramp" forced people to accept substitutes when they couldn't get the real thing. And besides, fans liked the idea that Luke didn't copy Charlie's gestures, only his clothes.

Starting in 1915 and running through most of 1917, "The Lonesome Luke" series made a tidy fortune for the Rolin Company (a name based upon the first letters of Roach and Dan Linthicum, Hal's business partner).

In the two years of the series, Lloyd made over a hundred Lonesome Luke pictures, which were billed as "Phunphilms," as bad a name as Hollywood has ever devised. To help his star clown, Roach hired Snub Pollard and Bebe Daniels.

Pollard was Lloyd's comic foil and he was magnificent in his absurd and hilarious get-ups, particularly his reversed Kaiser Wilhelm mustache. Before he finished his amazing career, Snub figured out that he had been doused by more than "ten tons of very wet cement . . . caught about fourteen thousand pies in his puss, and . . . had been hit by over six hundred automobiles and two trains."

Bebe Daniels played the heroine in Lloyd's films. The former stage actress was sixteen when she joined the Rolin Company, and during the four years she was with Roach made close to two hundred shorts. Following her comedy roles with Rolin, she moved over to Paramount, and her starring sex roles in Cecile B. DeMille pictures won her the reputation in the Twenties as "the screen's good-little bad girl." (Incidentally, she didn't help Zukor's censorship problems in 1922 when she was arrested for speeding and was sentenced to ten days in jail, with the press daily printing stories about her confinement.)

Everyone seemed pleased with the "Lonesome Luke" series but the most important person, Lloyd himself. By now he had grown to dislike copying someone else's style. Then, according to legend, one night in a movie theater in 1917 when Harold was watching himself on the screen he overheard a youngster explaining to his friend that this guy wasn't the real McCoy; he just imitated him. That settled it for Lloyd, and he decided to find himself a new role, even if it meant leaving Roach and Pathé.

Lloyd's idea was to find a screen image that was not only completely different from Chaplin's but also one that audiences could relate to. This new character, Harold theorized, had to get people pulling for him at the same time he was making them laugh.

The answer came to him one evening when he saw a film drama about an easy-going bespectacled minister who, when he got angry, took off his glasses and became a tough, two-fisted champion of justice. Except for the parson aspect of the character, the image fitted Harold's scheme perfectly. Here was the ordinary citizen whose quiet, everyday life and mild-mannered appearance masked a daring and dangerous-when-aroused hero. The key to the disguise was a pair of glasses, the human Clark Kent.

Lloyd's immediate problem was what kind of glasses his comedy figure should wear. Since the horned-rimmed kind had just become popular, he chose them instead of the more standard varieties. After experimenting with different sizes and weights, he bought a seventy-five-cent pair, took out the lenses so that light wouldn't bounce off them back into the camera, and wore "the magical glasses" for eighteen months before they finally broke. Unable to repair them, the shopkeeper wrote to the New York distributor and the manufacturer sent the comedian twenty-eight pairs for free in gratitude for the tremendous publicity Lloyd had given him.

Since he lacked the comic background that the other great clowns brought with them to film, Lloyd's "all-American" boy character developed slowly. From his childhood education, he drew upon his understanding of respectability; his hero was to be quiet, decent, well-mannered, and clean. The jokes had to come from the story not the costume. Exaggeration, carefully spaced and timed, would get the laughs, but all had to be tied to the audience's accepting the close resemblance between the comic figure and life itself.

Now the question was whether he could convince Roach and Pathé to let him switch roles. But his fears were short-lived. They agreed, and in late 1917 "The Glass Character," as Lloyd called him, was introduced to the public. So successful was the idea that two years later Pathé signed the comedian to a new contract and then revised it in 1920, giving Lloyd an estimated million and a half dollars, making him, many claimed, the highest-paid actor in the world.

There was, however, one period during those years when it looked as if Lloyd was through. On Sunday, August 24, 1919, he had agreed to have some publicity pictures made to advertise his new two-reelers. One of the poses required him to hold a fake bomb close to his cheek as a cigarette lighter. Somehow a real bomb got into the comedian's hand and he lit the fuse and started smoking his cigarette. Luckily, the photographer had to change plates and told Harold to relax with the bomb. Lloyd lowered his hand just as the thing exploded. Had he been holding it as the pose required, he would have been killed.

Almost a year passed before he was able to go back to work, and by this time a number of changes in movies were under way.

Roach, for example, had become less interested in directing Lloyd, preferring instead to let him write and direct his own films. Hal now became more involved with producing in general and emphasizing his particular brand of comedy movies, which featured strong story lines and clever predicaments rather than just zany sight gags. He also began bringing a number of famous personalities to the studio. Like Sennett, he had a knack for using other people's talents.

One marvelous personality he acquired was actor-director

Charley Chase. His pictures, based on simple but absurd plots, got their best laughs when Charley played the part of a harmless employee whose disasters at the office were only surpassed by his fights at home with his wife and mother.

Larry Semon, although on the decline when he came to Roach, still had a few good years left. So long as he stayed with his wild and fast-paced gags in short films, Semon rivaled Chaplin's popularity. His funniest comic creation, based upon a cartoon character he originated as a boy, was a silly fool wearing white clown makeup, small hat, sneakers, and high pants with wide suspenders. No matter what stupid situation he encountered, the prize sap just smiled and accepted the challenge.

A third popular comic that Roach imported to his lot was the great supporting character actor Jimmy Finlayson, whose greatest fame came in the sound era as the chief stooge in the Laurel and Hardy series. His specialty, when his screen anger wasn't wreaking havoc on someone or something, was the "double-take and fade-away." Jimmy was fond of looking at a situation, turning his attention elsewhere, then suddenly realizing just what he had seen and taking a second look, only this time with one eye squinting and the other growing wider.

Roach also, like Sennett, had a special insight into what makes people laugh. In 1922, for example, he still hadn't given up his idea for kid movies. Then one morning, according to Roach, a woman brought a child actress to audition for him, but he didn't think much of her ability and when they left he strolled to his window. Across the street was a lumber yard and he happened to see half a dozen children arguing. "They picked up these little strips of lumber that they'd cut off to make boards," Roach recalled, "and each one of them had five or six of these sticks. The largest one of these kids had this big stick, and the little kid claimed it. . . . All of a sudden, I realized for over fifteen minutes I'd listened to this silly argument over who owned these sticks . . . because these kids are real kids, they're on the square. They have no makeup; these are just kids being kids." And thus the idea for the "Our Gang" series was born.

Actually the name of the group was "The Little Rascals," but their first movie was called *Our Gang* and since the exhibitors kept asking for more "Our Gang" comedies, the name stuck.

The plots were almost always the same: a bunch of small-town kids get into trouble with adults or friends, become sick or lost, and go through the normal stages of growing up. Roach, for the most part, left the format of the series to his director Bob McGowan.

Over the next decade these delightful and amusing shorts became the training grounds for such memorable child stars as Jackie Cooper, Allan "Farina" Hoskins, and Nanette Fabray.

In these early years Roach had also begun collecting actors and directors who in the sound era were to become some of film's most famous personalities: Will Rogers, Stan Laurel, Oliver Hardy, Leo McCarey, and George Stevens. (Because their greatness rests with the "Talkies," their stories will not be discussed here.)

As Roach continued to change and grow artistically so did Lloyd and the movie industry. By 1912, he had gone as far as he could with two-reelers. What's more, his "glass" character had become familiar to movie-goers around the world. They particularly enjoyed the special "thrills" that the comedian interjected in a number of his two-reelers. The popular story featured Harold as a likeable young man starting out in business, from the bottom up. But he was a go-getter and sometimes it got him into trouble with bosses and bullies and his screen sweetheart (by now Mildred Davis). Before he won out, the glass hero often had to perform some daring feat like climbing a tall building, and the dangers faced by him often caused the audience first to gasp at his awkward attempts and then laugh at his amazing success. Although people like Douglas Fairbanks and Larry Semon used thrill effects in their comedy routines, no one was ever as capable as Lloyd of manufacturing the pace and timing of these remarkable visual gags.

But by 1922 the theater owners and fans were paying the best prices for feature-length films and the era of the great comedy shorts was drawing slowly to an end. All the famous comics were making longer movies and Lloyd's last two intended two-reelers had somehow grown into four- and five-reelers. So he decided that was where his future lay. Then, in his second feature picture, he made one of the great comedy movies.

The idea for *Safety Last* came to him one afternoon when he stopped in downtown Los Angeles to observe Bill Strothers, who billed himself as the Human Spider, scale the side of a large office building. So nervous did Lloyd get that at one point he was frightened to look up at Strothers.

Around that experience the film star designed a comedy about a farm boy who comes to the big city and finds a job clerking in a department store. Soon he makes enemies with the floor manager and when the "human fly" that the store owners have hired for a publicity stunt can't appear, Lloyd is forced to take his place and scale the steep side of a skyscraper.

What makes the film so marvelous is Lloyd's exceptional skill in mixing chuckles with chills. Even more exciting than the story itself is the fact that except in one or two rare shots, Harold performed the dangerous stunts himself. Of course, he admitted that for the first few days he was scared stiff.

With the completion of *Safety Last,* Roach and Lloyd agreed to separate. It was a friendly parting that came about mainly over studio space. The Roach lot was crowded and Harold, now ready like Chaplin to run his own affairs, decided it best to release his pictures through Paramount's giant distributing organization. At the same time he decided the best way to keep his leading lady was to marry her, and they remained married all his life.

It was about a year later that director McGowan hired an unknown gag man to help him with the "Our Gang" series. Frank Capra may well have been the first brilliant comedy writer-director with a college degree, especially one in engineering. But in other respects he fitted perfectly into Hollywood's traditional past.

Born May 18, 1898 to poor, struggling Italian peasants, he immigrated to America when he was six years of age and suffered the scorn and abuse of his relatives and friends when his parents made it possible for at least one of their seven children to get a college education. By 1924, when he came to Roach, Capra had worked at dozens of different jobs and decided to throw in his fortunes with movies.

But Frank never got to meet Roach in the six months he was at the studio. The producer, an easy-going genius who gave others a chance to grow on their own, left McGowan alone and he, in turn, kept Capra away from the set where the children were shooting. Bob felt that visitors on the set made the kids nervous so he daily met Frank for lunch and it was then that the writer gave the director the new gags.

Capra knew full well that these arrangements could only be temporary. After all, what did a tough city kid know about writing gags for easy-going country rubes. Besides, the pay was bad and he had no office to work in. But this last aspect turned out to be a break for Frank. Will Rogers took a liking to him and offered Capra his dressing room as a place to write. He also kept Frank stuffed with doughnuts and coffee.

After six months of "Our Gang" work, Capra decided to tackle the big time, Mack Sennett himself. So he coaxed Rogers to set up an interview for the new job.

Now you just didn't get to see the great producer in his tower if you were looking for a job. Instead, Frank met with the chief writers who offered him the standard beginning salary of thirty-five dollars, five dollars less than he was making at Roach's. Capra refused. Rather than lose him, the interviewer brought the brash young man to Mack Sennett, who, not surprisingly, was nude and getting a rubdown at the time. The deal was finalized when Capra showed Sennett how both men could save face. Mack could hire the newcomer at the set salary and the next day give him a ten-dollar raise.

It didn't take long for the clever college graduate to impress the crafty Sennett, who in 1924 was a millionaire many times over and had traded his horse for a flashy Rolls-Royce. Then one day, Mack told Capra that he wanted him to look at a film that had been made of a second-rate vaudeville act, featuring a baby-faced comic. Frank, along with the others who had seen the stage clown, felt that Sennett was dead wrong on the man's comic ability. But they were dealing with the King of Comedy and once more he had discovered a great star.

Lloyd began his comedy career by imitating other clowns. Here is a scene from one of the many "Lonesome Luke" comedies made in 1915. Harold is in the middle.

Lloyd's first feature film, "Grandma's Boy" (1922), had him play an insecure youth who learns to believe in himself.

*In "Safety Last" (1923), Harold began to use thrill comedy. His
specialty became comedy from way up high.*

In "Why Worry?" (1923), Harold played the part of a rich man who goes to Mexico to find a cure for an imaginary illness and is mistaken for a spy. Jahan Aasen plays the giant Mexican.

Lloyd once more played the shy, bashful hero who needed some self-confidence in the 1925 classic "The Freshman."

*The idea of the small-town hero making good
we see the determined Lloyd saving the*

became the basic idea in Lloyd's comedies. Here
game for his college in "The Freshman."

VI

The Last of the Great Clowns HARRY LANGDON

The two-reeler that Capra and the other writers watched that late afternoon was called *Harry's New Car* and starred a husband-and-wife team. The man was a small, wide-eyed, baby-faced fellow with chubby features and his name was Harry Langdon. The bit consisted of his car getting wrecked while his mean wife screamed at him and he acted foolish and helpless all the time.

When the lights went on in the screening room, the writers stared at each other in dismay. After all, the ex-vaudevillian was almost forty, had been in show business for most of his life and still was a nobody. Of the two-reelers he had made none had shown any merit and why the boss still thought he was good was a mystery. Besides, Arthur Sterling, one of the writers, remarked that heaven was the only place to get help for Harry. It was at that moment, according to Capra, that he got the brilliant idea to create Langdon's famous clown with child-like faith. "Where's the comedy in Chaplin?" Frank asked. "It's in his character, the little tramp. Harry'll be the Little Elf." Afterwards, the gag men spent their remaining time devising the theory of a funny character who was too naive to see things as they really were. Instead, he went innocently along life's difficult journey, not bothering anyone and hoping they'd do the same for him.

The next step was to convince Sennett that Ripley and Capra should stick close to Langdon. The boss's rule was that writers, directors, and actors didn't mix. But this was a special case since the star didn't know where his real talent was; Mack agreed and the new team was formed, with Harry Edwards assigned the directing chores.

Within two years Langdon was as famous as Chaplin, Keaton, and Lloyd, and in just as many years he was a nobody. Why? What happened to give him the most spectacular ride up and down the ladder of success?

The great pantomimist was born on June 15, 1884, in Council Bluffs, Iowa, to poor parents who worked for the Salvation Army. By the time he was twelve, Harry was fed up with poverty and small-town life and ran away from home to join a traveling medicine show. Afterwards, he made the usual beginner's appearances in circuses, stock companies, and burlesque. Finally in 1903 Langdon was good enough to have his own act called "Johnny's New Car." His idea of comedy was to sit on stage in a small, wooden break-away car that had gotten stuck in front of a hospital. He tried to repair the engine but it exploded and before the inept "mechanic" had finished, the car had been destroyed, piece by piece. The character in the routine over the years began to develop into an innocent and sappy soul unable to cope in a mature way with his daily problems. It was great pantomime but weak comedy.

By 1923 when Principal Pictures Corporation gave him a movie contract and filmed his vaudeville act, Harry had not made much of a career for himself. Even after his two-bit movie company unloaded him on Sennett, Langdon still didn't show any signs of improving. But Mack believed in the bland comic and now was willing to try the "baby-faced clown" idea.

More than anything else the credit goes to the behind-the-scenes trio who worked for Langdon and the material they developed. First came the transformation in his screen image. As Capra described it in his autobiography, *The Name Above the Title,* "Langdon himself was at heart a child in real life. Now a child can be bratty, whiny, sulky, cruel. We gave the character the 'fix' that made him appealing—a grown man with the actions and reactions of a trusting *innocent* child." This elevated Langdon's figure to a more universal appeal, putting him on the same high level as the other great comedians. Capra explained it in these terms, "Chaplin *thought* his way out of tight situations; Keaton *suffered* through them stoically; Lloyd overcame them with *speed*. But Langdon *trusted* his way through adversities, surviving only with the help of God or goodness."

Along with the screen hero's trust came a peaceful state of mind that refused to consider any violence. In moments of danger, Langdon looked and acted as if he wasn't aware that he was in trouble and thus, by a simple but honest faith in heaven, he escaped. One of his best techniques in these situations was a "triple-take." Twice he'd face his problem and twice he'd turn away, still not realizing fully the trouble he was in, and then slowly, as if waking from a dream, he'd get the picture and the third look frightened him out of his wits. But here again, an essential part of the baby-faced hero was that no evil thoughts crossed his mind. If misfortune came his way his innocence and faith would protect him and somehow the danger would pass.

Another key "gag" in Langdon's infantile image was his relationship with women. He usually played a guy about to be married or a henpecked husband too simple to recognize his slavery. In either case, women frightened him. That is, he wanted to be close with them but wasn't quite sure how or why or what was the best way to handle the relationship. For that matter, he never seemed to know just what sex, in general, was all about.

Overnight, Langdon became a sensation. But his tragic flaw was pride. He never considered anyone but himself and foolishly thought he alone was responsible for his sudden fame. Sennett, in his autobiography, *King of Comedy,* described the situation best, "Under Frank's easy guidance Harry soon became a Keystone star in two-reel comedies. His salary went up to several thousand dollars a week. Langdon became important and unfortunately realized it. Suddenly he forgot that all his value lay in being that baby-witted boy on the screen. His cunning as a businessman was about that of a backward kindergarten student and he complicated this by marital adventures, in which he was about as inept as he was on the screen."

By 1925, Harry was so in love with himself that no one was able to control him. He felt that if he could make so much money for Sennett he could make even more for himself, alone. Lloyd and Chaplin had their own companies and he wanted his own too. He didn't have to wait very long either. When First National made him an offer, he accepted, getting from them an advance of $150,000. He used a good deal of the cash to help persuade Ripley, Capra, and Edwards to join his new company.

His insecurity about his own status compared with that of the other famous clowns intensified when two of the greatest comedy films ever made appeared in 1925.

Chaplin's *The Gold Rush* premiered in August. It is the story of the little tramp as a lone prospector for gold in the dangerous Klondike. Clearly ill-prepared and incompetent, yet without fear or doubt, Charlie sets out to find his fortune. Very soon he gets himself into a small, remote cabin with two giant-size men, and all three are in danger of dying from starvation.

It is at this point that Chaplin created one of the most ingenious comic scenes in film history. Having drawn straws, one member of the trio leaves in search of food. The remaining two, Chaplin and Mack Swain, become so desperate that Charlie prepares a feast by cooking his boot. The illusion that laces are spaghetti, nails delicious bones, and a shoe's sole a rare piece of meat is a classic of genuine comic art.

But the danger passes and the two men separate, the third man being killed by divine justice for his crimes. Charlie comes to a tough boom town and falls in love with the beautiful dance hall queen, who finds the shabby little fellow a great source of amusement. He misunderstands her attentions to him and invites Georgia and her friends to a New Year's Eve party at his tiny cabin. That evening as he waits in vain, he dreams about the lovely party he would have had and does his memorable pantomime of the dance of the rolls, another brilliant moment in film history.

Shortly after the dismal party experience he again meets Swain, who having been hit on the head, has lost his memory and with it the location of his gold mine. Mack promises to share his fortunes with Charlie if the little fellow will take him back to the cabin where they once spent the lonely winter. From there the big man could locate his claim. After a side-splitting scene at the fragile cabin, the gold mine is found, they become millionaires, and Chaplin gets his girl.

It was the master clown at his best and it was his use of pathos that so captivated Langdon, who thereafter insisted that Capra and the others devise more heart-rending scenes for him in his pictures.

A month later Lloyd released his great comedy, *The Freshman*. In this wild and hilarious spoof of college football films, Harold played his typical Horatio Alger hero—a young, clean-cut kid who against his father's will decides to go to college, get an education, and eventually makes good.

His first weeks of school give Lloyd a chance to satirize the hazing of newcomers as well as the weak attempts to make friends among the student body. But soon "the glass character" meets a lovely co-ed and realizes that the only way to win her heart is to play football. He goes out for the team which he clearly appears ill-suited to make. The sight gags of Harold going through practice and scrimmages are superb, particularly when he becomes the team's tackling dummy.

Eventually the day of the big game arrives and to the surprise of no one in the audience Harold gets sent in, but only after all other reserves have been physically injured. By using suspense in the actual game's outcome, the clever star gave his fans their usual "thrill" effects before he succeeded in winning the game and the girl.

Never again did Lloyd achieve such comic genius as in *The Freshman*. After 1938, he left the industry and spent most of his remaining years a very happy and successful man who had given the world some of its funniest moments.

Two other events in 1925 that Langdon evidenced little concern over but are of interest to us involved old acquaintances of ours. The first dealt with Max Linder, the first famous clown. After Chaplin left Essanay, the demand for more comics like him convinced George Spoor (the "S" in Essanay) to go to Europe and bring Linder back to the movies. After all, Chaplin, in a rare moment of modesty, had once claimed that Linder was his model at the start. Max, still weak, but eager to work again, agreed and in 1917 began a series of comedies at Spoor's Chicago studio. But they were doomed from the start. Weather, language problems, meddling film executives, and bad health only made Linder's attempts seem pathetic and misguided. Following the third short he canceled his contract by mutual consent with Spoor and returned to Paris.

Two years later, however, he came back to the United States, somewhat at Chaplin's encouragement, set up his own producing company, and began to make a number of very good comedy feature-length films, which unfortunately did not succeed with the public. Not even his developing close friendship with Chaplin and other famous stars could offset his frequent states of depression, and these mental problems soon affected his production schedule and output. Without warning he sold his holdings in America and returned to France in 1922.

The following year he married and in June of 1925 the tragic couple had a baby girl. Four months later on the night of October 30th, the sad clown who claimed he had nothing to live for, convinced his young wife to join him in a suicide pact and they killed themselves.

The second event that year sounded the death bell for all of silent films. After every major studio had turned them down, Western Electric convinced Warner Brothers to begin making sound films, the first of which were to be released in 1926.

But in 1926, Langdon was more excited over the enthusiastic press reaction that his first feature-length film, *Tramp,*

Tramp, Tramp, was getting. Harry played the part of a penniless son who needed money for his sick father's operation and therefore set out to win the prize money being offered by a millionaire shoe manufacturer in a cross-country walking race.

One interesting aspect of the film was the publicity for the race. Twenty-four sheet billboard posters along the route displayed pictures of the rich man's daughter who was to crown the winner. Eventually Harry and the daughter accidently meet, but in shooting the scene the actress who was new to the movies just couldn't stop laughing at Harry's funny, hesitant, and awkward gestures as he recognized her face on the posters. Over and over again, the scene had to be reshot until the girl learned not to laugh but play her part straight. By the time the shooting was finished, Joan Crawford was a mental and physical mess.

More than one critic agreed with *The New York Times* reviewer that while Langdon was good, he seemed very similar in a number of scenes to Chaplin. As the reviewer stated it, "While viewing Harry Langdon in his first feature length production . . . one is impelled to feel a greater respect for Charlie Chaplin's genius than ever, for although Mr. Langdon undoubtedly has a keen sense of the ridiculous there are in this new film several episodes that are strongly reminiscent of *The Gold Rush* and which suffer by comparison with the Chaplin comedy."

Disregarding Capra's and other people's advice, Langdon insisted on bringing his comic image more and more in line with the pathos of the little tramp. But in his next and greatest film Harry proved that if only he had left the thinking to others he would have stayed at the top for a long, long time.

The Strong Man, released four months later, had one clever bit after another. In this remarkable movie the baby-faced hero is a Belgian soldier captured during World War I by a huge German. After the Armistice, he comes to the United States as an assistant to the German, who now calls himself Zandow the Great. Harry is determined to find his "pen-pal" who wrote to him during the war but is unaware that Mary Brown is blind or that it is a common American name. Langdon superbly plays up the trouble of finding the right girl and at one point indulges in a magnificent scene with a vamp who is out to "take" the timid little man.

By chance on the way to the right town, Harry has a masterly bit of business that adds little to the story line but stands out in film comedy as a classic example of what one individual with just a bad cold can do to get laughs. His incredible pantomime of an innocent, wistful clown whose homemade cures so arouse his fellow passengers that they are willing to commit murder is slapstick humor at its best.

In the end, of course, he wins the girl but not before he miraculously cleans up the wicked town. Interestingly enough, Chaplin, five years later, imitated Langdon when in *City Lights* the little tramp fell in love with a blind girl.

The Strong Man nevertheless had several flaws, typical of most silent comedies. The narrative rambled and the best parts were in gags not really involved with the story itself.

Everyone praised the film, but now people began questioning who deserved the credit, Langdon or the man who directed the film, Frank Capra. (Edwards had gotten fed up with Harry's ego trip and quit.) You can just imagine how Langdon felt about someone else getting "his" praise.

Work began almost immediately on the next film, *Long Pants,* a story about a country rube who finds himself in trouble with city slickers and a love triangle with a home-town girl and a gangster's moll.

But by now Langdon made it a point of publicly taking credit for his character and his films while at the same time widening the gulf between Capra and himself. It got so bad that at one point he refused to cooperate with his writer-director and told him so in public. Capra then followed Langdon to his dressing room and told the stupid man exactly what the "gang" thought of his ungrateful behavior. Later that night a friend rang Capra's doorbell, and embarrassed, gave him a check, saying that Langdon had fired Capra, the man who made him a star. The irate clown wouldn't even let Capra edit the film, which was released in 1927 and received rave reviews.

Frank Capra survived the incident and for the next forty years went on to become one of the screen's greatest directors, making such outstanding pictures as *It Happened One Night* (the only film ever to earn Academy Awards for every major category), *Mr. Deeds Goes to Town, State of the Union,* and *Lost Horizon.*

As for Harry Langdon, with Capra and Edwards gone, he became a nothing. His attempt at directing, writing and acting in his own films was a disaster, and two pictures later his corporation was dissolved.

In December, 1944, Harry was making a cheap two-reeler when he was stricken with severe head pains which foreshadowed the cerebral hemorrhage that caused his death two weeks later. Langdon never understood what had happened to cause the public to love him one day and turn against him the next.

Silent film fans saw their last great comedy movie in 1927 when Buster Keaton appeared in *The General.* This time the dead-pan genius played the part of Johnny Gray, the brave little conductor of an important rebel train called "The General" which is stolen by Yankee spies. The sad, small man finds that the woman he loves, who thinks of him as a coward, has also been kidnapped by mistake.

Keaton, in his continuous efforts to out-do his sight gags,

never surpassed those moments in this film when he took up the pursuit of the captured locomotive. As always it came down to a chase between the stoical clown and the mighty machine, and the intricate gags plus his masterly acrobatics may well place Keaton's performance here as the single greatest act in silent film comedy. We must keep in mind that Keaton often had to work twice as hard as other clowns to get laughs because he never changed his facial expression. The film itself was not as fast-paced as his others, and many people, although they liked the acrobatic artistry, wished for a movie totally committed to clowning.

Eight months later Al Jolson starred in the Warner Brothers' film *The Jazz Singer* and talking pictures became the rage.

With the coming of sound, Keaton found life more and more unbearable at M-G-M. Restrictions and interference, marital problems and alcoholism, all contributed to his downfall, and starting in 1933 his life became a nightmare filled with divorces, straight-jackets, and humiliation. A mild comeback in the early Fifties helped restore some of his youthful fame, and he died in 1966 once more aware that the world appreciated his great art.

As for Sennett, the story was almost as bad. The man who made millions lost it all in the Depression and wound up his days mostly forgotten by the world he had given so much to in terms of joy and laughter.

Looking back on those voiceless days when aggressive immigrants and refugees from poverty row bounded together to form a new art for people everywhere, you sometimes wonder if it was all worth it. And then you remember that yesterday's clowns were a rare breed, and the best any of us can say is that we are better off for their having graced the silver screen.

One of the most forgotten clowns of yesteryear was the memorable "white-faced" Larry Semon, shown here in his last film, "Spuds" (1928). He died this same year, at thirty-nine, bankrupt and friendless.

Hal Roach, Sennett's greatest rival.

By the late 1920's, Roach had the most successful comedy team from "Big Business" (1929), Oliver is holding Stan back from

*in Hollywood—Oliver Hardy and Stan Laurel. In this scene
biting the ear of the great comic stooge James Finlayson.*

By far, Roach's greatest success after Lloyd in the twenties was his creation of the Little Rascals. Sitting on the steps from top to bottom, left to right, Mickey Daniels, Johnny Downs, Kacloe Condon, Joe Cobb, Mary Kornman, Jackie Davis, and Allan "Farina" Hoskins.

Here are some more of the Little Rascals shown with their
director, Bob McGowan. Left to right are Tommy Bond,
Dorothy DeBorba, Pete the Pup, Baby Spanky, Director
McGowan, Baby Georgie Stevens, Jr., and "Stymie" Beard.

Sennett's last great discovery in the twenties was the ex-vaudevillian

Harry Langdon. He is shown here with his wife, Rose, in their famous car act.

Langdon, the shy, childish clown, appeared in this 1924 Sennett two-reeler entitled "Feet of Mud."

Edgar Kennedy, another Roach favorite, is credited with popularizing the "slow burn," the method of taking a brief moment before reacting angrily to an insult.

In 1934, Director Frank Capra (left) along with his stars Claudette Colbert and Clark Gable all won Academy Awards for their work in "It Happened One Night." The film is the only one in movie history which got every major award, including picture of the year and best screen play.

The Three Keatons, the popular vaudeville act of 1900; from left to right: Buster, Joe, and Myra.

Chaplin in the famous dinner scene from "The Gold Rush,"
where Charlie uses a shoestring for spaghetti and a shoe's sole
for meat.

Lloyd in "The Freshman," suggesting that all you need to succeed in life is faith in yourself.

Langdon, the sad, pathetic clown in "The Strong Man" (1926).

Chaplin, the greatest clown of them all, in "The Gold Rush."
The girl is Georgia Hale.

BIBLIOGRAPHY

The author hopes that the following selective book list will help the interested reader to explore more fully the history of the silent clowns. Because of this book's brevity, only a few writers' opinions were singled out, and for that reason extensive references to specific authors have not been given. Anyone reading the following material, which the author has consulted, will have no difficulty in determining which books were made use of, what was taken from them, and where each went his own way.

BOOKS

Blesch, Rudi. *Keaton*. New York: The Macmillan Company, 1966.

Brownlow, Kevin. *The Parade's Gone By*. New York: Alfred A. Knopf, 1968.

Cahn, William. *Harold Lloyd's World of Comedy*. New York: Duell, Sloan, and Pearce, 1964.

————. *The Laugh Makers: A Pictorial History of American Comedians*. New York: G. P. Putnam's Sons, 1957.

Capra, Frank. *The Name Above the Title*. New York: The Macmillan Company, 1971.

Chaplin, Charles. *My Autobiography*. New York: Simon and Schuster, 1964.

Chaplin, Charles, Jr., with N. and M. Rau. *My Father, Charlie Chaplin*. New York: Popular Library, 1961.

Corio, Ann, with Joseph DiMona. *This Was Burlesque*. New York: Grosset and Dunlap, 1968.

Cotes, Peter, and Thelma Niklaus. *The Little Fellow: The Life and Works of Charles Spencer Chaplin*. New York: Philosophical Library, 1951.

Crowther, Bosley. *The Great Films: Fifty Golden Years of Motion Pictures*. New York: G. P. Putnam's Sons, 1967.

DeMille, Cecil B., with Donald Hayne. *Autobiography*. Englewood Cliffs: Prentice-Hall, 1959.

Durgnat, Raymond. *The Crazy Mirror: Hollywood Comedy and the American Image*. New York: Horizon Press, 1969.

Everson, William K. *The Films of Hal Roach*. New York: The Museum of Modern Art, 1971.

Feibleman, James K. *In Praise of Comedy: A Study in Its Theory and Practice*. New York: Horizon Press, 1970.

Fowler, Gene. *Father Goose: The Story of Mack Sennett*. New York: Covici, Friede Publishers, 1934.

Franklin, Joe. *Classics of the Silent Screen: A Pictorial Treasury*. New York: Branhall House, 1959.

French, Philip. *The Movie Moguls: An Informal History of the Hollywood Tycoons*. London: Weidenfeld and Nicolson, 1969.

Green, Abel, and Joe Laurie, Jr. *Show Biz: From Vaude to Video*. New York: Henry Holt and Company, 1951.

Griffith, Richard, and Arthur Mayer. *The Movies*. Revised edition. New York: Simon and Schuster, 1970.

Huff, Theodore. *Charlie Chaplin*. New York: Henry Schuman, 1951.

Jacobs, Lewis. *The Rise of the American Film; A Critical History*. New York: Harcourt, Brace and Company, 1939.

Keaton, Buster, and Charles Samuels. *My Wonderful World of Slapstick*. New York: Doubleday and Company, 1960.

Lahue, Kalton C. *Mack Sennett's Keystone: The Man, the Myth and the Comedies*. New York: A. S. Barnes and Company, 1971.

———. *World of Laughter: The Motion Picture Comedy Short, 1910–1930*. Norman: University of Oklahoma Press, 1966.

——— and Terry Brewer. *Kops and Kustards: The Legend of Keystone Films*. Norman: University of Oklahoma Press, 1967.

——— and Sam Gill. *Clown Princes and Court Jesters: Some*

Great Comics of the Silent Screen. New York: A. S. Barnes and Company, 1970.

Laurie, Joe, Jr. *Vaudeville: From the Honky-Tonks to the Palace*. New York: Henry Holt and Company, 1953.

Lebel, J. P. *Buster Keaton*. New York: A. S. Barnes and Company, 1967.

Lloyd, Harold, and Wesley W. Stout. *An American Comedy*. New York: Benjamin Blom, 1971. First published in 1928.

Manchel, Frank. *When Pictures Began to Move*. Englewood Cliffs: Prentice-Hall, 1969.

————. *Cameras West*. Englewood Cliffs: Prentice-Hall, 1969.

Mast, Gerald. *A Short History of the Movies*. New York: Pegasus, 1971.

McCaffrey, Donald W. *4 Great Comedians: Chaplin, Lloyd, Keaton, Langdon*. New York: A. S. Barnes and Company, 1968.

————, editor. *Focus on Chaplin*. Englewood Cliffs: Prentice-Hall, 1971.

McDonald, Gerald D., et al., editors. *The Films of Charlie Chaplin*. New York: Bonanza Books, 1965.

McLean, Albert F., Jr. *American Vaudeville as Ritual*. Lexington: University of Kentucky Press, 1965.

Montgomery, John. *Comedy Films*. London: George Allen and Unwin, 1954.

Payne, Robert. *The Great God Pan: A Biography of the Tramp Played by Charles Chaplin*. New York: Hermitage House, 1952.

Quigly, Isabel. *Charlie Chaplin: Early Comedies*. New York: E. P. Dutton and Company, 1968.

Robinson, David. *Buster Keaton*. Bloomington: Indiana University Press, 1969.

————. *The Great Funnies: A History of Film Comedy*. Bloomington: Indiana University Press, 1969.

Sennett, Mack, and Cameron Shepp. *King of Comedy*. New York: Doubleday and Company, 1954.

Sobel, Bernard. *A Pictorial History of Burlesque*. New York: Bonanza Books, 1956.

————. *A Pictorial History of Vaudeville*. New York: The Citadel Press, 1961.

Talbot, Daniel, editor. *Film: An Anthology*. New York: Simon and Schuster, 1959.

Tyler, Parker. *Chaplin: Last of the Clowns*. New York: The Vanguard Press, 1948.

ARTICLES

Agee, James. "Comedy's Greatest Era," *Life,* 27 (September 5, 1949), 70–88.

Bishop, Christopher. "The Great Stone Face" and "An Interview with Buster Keaton," *Film Quarterly,* 12 (Fall, 1958), 10–22.

Bodeen, DeWitt. "Bebe Daniels," *Films in Review,* 15 (August–September, 1964), 413–30.

Friedman, Arthur B. "Interview with Harold Lloyd," *Film Quarterly,* 15 (Summer, 1962), 7–13.

Garringer, Nelson E. "Harold Lloyd," *Films in Review,* 13 (August–September, 1962), 407–22.

Gilliatt, Penelope. "Buster Keaton," *Film 70–71,* edited by David Denby. New York: Simon and Schuster, 1971. Pp. 269–76.

Giroux, Robert. "Mack Sennett: Part One," *Films in Review,* 19 (December, 1968), 593–612.

————. "Mack Sennett: Part Two," *Films in Review,* 19 (January, 1969), 1–28.

Schonert, Vernon L. "Harry Langdon," *Films in Review,* 18 (October, 1967), 470–85.

Slide, Anthony. "Hal Roach on Film Comedy," *The Silent Picture,* 6 (Spring, 1970), 2–7.

————. "Harold Lloyd Talks About His Early Career," *The Silent Picture,* 7 (Summer–Autumn, 1971), 4–8.

Spears, Jack. "Max Linder," *Films in Review,* 16 (May, 1965), 272–91.

INDEX

152